Uncommon Poems
Common People

by T.D. Kruser

DORRANCE
PUBLISHING CO
EST. 1920
PITTSBURGH, PENNSYLVANIA 15238

Dorrance Publishing Co
585 Alpha Drive
Suite 103
Pittsburgh, PA 15238
Visit our website at *www.dorrancebookstore.com*

ISBN: 978-1-6470-2549-6
eISBN: 978-1-6470-2678-3

Contents

I. The Edge

Prologue

People

People...
    I watch, and I listen,
        And I wait for them to let a piece of themselves go;
And I grab it, save it,
    For it is a precious thing.
Writing is my way of retaining it
      So that someday it may
        Come back to them.

The Edge

We leave the simplicities of childhood, step onto the ledge of life.
    We challenge the outside, not knowing what is there.
        We face the world.

As each day passes,
    Our lives gradually merge with those around us;
And before we know it
    We are all entangled, caught in each other's spells.

We join and part, and join, and part,
    And join...and part.
In time's passing, through others we gather
    Reflections of ourselves and hide them inside.

For each of us there comes a day
    When we stop long enough to look in our mirrors
      And see all around us,
The worlds of our emotions
    Which we feel but cannot touch.
We find ourselves insecure and unknowing
    In a world that once seemed so familiar;
We find ourselves,
    On The Edge.

Joy in Love

Quest

The search for a lifemate is a dream of youth;
>An end, a beginning,
>>We claim as our right.

We plan, we dream,
>We connive, and we scheme;
Through every waking day,
>Through every sleepless night.

And we watch, and we listen,
>And we shine—
>>Our—
>>>Light.

Discover Me

The first day I met you,
>I thought you could be the one.
The next time I talked to you,
>I felt we had begun.
I want to know you,
>I want you to know me.
I'd like for us to share,
>To see if it could be
Our chance for love;
>Discover me.

Quietly

Skies still and blue, walking here with you;
    The smile in your eyes telling me it's all right.
It unsettles me, how quiet you are;
    I'm so unsure, how near or how far,
        I should go to discover the real you inside.
You're waiting for me to speak what you need to hear,
    To tell you what's on my mind.
I ponder on just the right words to say,
    I fear the wrong ones might send you away;
        I struggle with what I can't find.
Instead, I quietly hold your hand
    And in its warmth let you feel my heart.

Ours (New Love)

Darling, give me love;
    That's warm, that's soft, that's ours.
Let us hold and touch more tightly;
    Saying nothing, merely believing
        This is love.

We are here
    In the silence of the night.
        The moon shines down;
Its light revealing the passion we're feeling.
    My love, your love; ours only.

The time for love is now and it knows no end.
Hours together, touching forever;
Our love.

Our hearts know, our minds ask,
If this is all there is;
Me, you, our love together?
Our uncertain smiles reflect our souls,
Our gentle tears, they let us know
Love; it is ours.

Love

There's something reassuring
In the feeling of being loved
And all that it entails.

Trust and intimacy,
Never doubting;
Always having peace.

Joy untold forever,
Comfort wearing a smile;
Believing in our love.

My desire is to simply express
The feelings of my heart.
I love you.

Security

My depth, my utter soul of joy,
 Cries out with your touch.
Your serene beauty, your vibrancy;
 Make me feel…. I fall into my heart.

Hold me forever, dear love.
 My shelter is your smile;
  My days are days of joy.

In your eternal sunshine
 My loneliness cries,
My soul rejoices…
 I find peace in your arms.

Best of Both Worlds

Talk and touch,
 I care for you much;
  Kiss and hug my one true love.
It feels so fine living through time,
 And sharing all that makes up
  The best of both worlds.

You're my friend, it's your closeness I treasure;
 In the arms of my love, it's excitement and pleasure.

I live the dreams of a man twice fulfilled,
 Sharing the best of both loves, the best of both worlds.

Talk and touch,
 You care for me much;
  Kiss and hug your one true love.
Isn't it fine to live through a time
 In which we can share
  The best of both worlds?

Yes, we're friends, it's our closeness we treasure.
 For both kinds of love, therein lies the measure
Of the truth of our souls, of two hearts fulfilled,
 Sharing the best of both loves, the best of both worlds.

Intimate Moment

Gentle mist, cool mist,
 Drawing beads of crystal on your soft, dark hair.
Visions of perfection wished,
 In the smell of your skin in the cool night air.
Reaching forth, feather wings,
 Your fingertips touch my arm.
Secure in this, feelings kissed,
 I protect thee from all harm;
  For I love you.

Waiting

Can't you tell it just to look at me,
    Can you see it in my eyes?
The feelings hiding deep inside,
    Those things I can't disguise.
I'll tell you to your face, my dear,
    So you can know it's true;
I've found someone I've waited for,
    And that someone, love, is you.

Oh, yes, dear, I've been waiting,
    Through summer day and moonlit night;
Just waiting for that special love,
    The one that's meant for me, just right.
I've been waiting for so long
    For the love that I've been due;
Just waiting for my life to begin,
    Love, now it's begun with you.

Now you know what it's all about,
    I'm waiting for your reply.
Remember, dear, I love you so,
    My heart can tell you why.
You've said yes, I can only say
    That's all I've ever dreamed of.
We've found that something waited for,
    And that something, dear, is love.

On the Road

Across the miles I travel to do what I must do.
    Though I'm not there, don't stop to care,
        For my heart is home with you.

This morning starts another day like the one that passed before.
    Remember, dear, though you're not here,
        I love you all the more.

My heart, it holds your memory, but it's you for whom I yearn.
    Please wait for me, soon it will be
        The time for my return;
And we can hold, and touch,
    And love again.

Rejoining

Soaring on wings through misty cloud,
    with the sun reflecting, shining bright on
    the blue-white horizon; heading home.
You, my love, wait for me; impatiently stroking
    your brown chestnut hair with eager fingertips,
    waiting for the moment to come when you
    are in my arms again.

I, your love, sit back and think of the last time
    I held your tender, warm body in my arms;
    needing for the moment to come again to
    share in the security of your warmth.
Time, the many lonely moments that pass by,
    unconscious of our need. Yet, in its passing,
    bringing us closer to the moments we will
    share again.
We, filled with the intense excitement of
    our growing need for each other and the
    imminence of our joining, look out onto
    that blue-white horizon and wonder at the gift
    given us; of the beauty of our love.

Separation, Loneliness, and Despair

Hands

I hold your heart, my love;
    With my hands I give it care.
From my heart I feed it warmth;
    Of my soul, my all.

I hold your letter, dear love.
    In my palms, bitter there;
Shaking hands, my soul is bared.
    I make believe I don't care.

You held my heart, dear love;
    In your hands it felt secure.
Now betrayed, now unsure,
    Only lies…bleeding.

Song of Love, Lost

Love—Sand in the wind,
    Shattered crystal, torn silk.
Love—I gave you forever;
    An existence, a soul.
Love—You gave me never;
    A blossom shorn, eclipsed sunlight.
Love—I try to hold on, frozen motionless;

Tethered still to a restless moon.
Love—Breath of fading song,
    A valley too far, too distant;
        All too quickly passed.
Love—A waterfall drains itself without cease within me;
    My mind and heart are the weight of lead.
        Why did you leave?

Hard Truth

I'm always too late to say sorry;
    Never to expect you to love me again.
The truth is hard, they're heard to say;
    I have no cause to differ.

My depth of love so hard to fathom…
    My mind cannot accept
What my heart tells me so;
    I must.

My greatest sorrow can only be
    That it should have never been;
No one understands,
    Never—so it is.

With a troubled heart and soul;
    But for to ease my mind
I must accept
    Even my own bitter thoughts.

Better to be out of touch,
   Than in reach and out of love.
      Goodbye, forever.

If

If a life could be forgotten or memories swept away,
   I wouldn't have to cry.
If my heart could be read or the past relived
   It might not be such a painful goodbye.
If wishes were dreams and dreams come true,
   I would know what to say.
If people are stone and feelings glass,
   Why do I find myself so shattered today?

You Were Mine

In the quiet night I still hear the memories,
   My dreams, they keep me from sleep;
I feel the weight of the years passed behind me,
   My empty hands hold the rewards I reap.
I remember you once were mine;
   I thought that you were mine.

Your lips said I was special,
   Your eyes said you were mine.

And my mind said you were my dream come true
    And your touch was, oh, so fine.
I felt much more than I was,
    What a special act we played;
It wasn't just a one-night stand,
    Just another closing day.
I thought that you were mine;
    You were mine.

All I asked was to not live with love unknown.
    All I wanted was to hold you,
        Take you home; be mine alone.
But it was too high a price to pay for you to give to me.
        Your freedom was the only thing you loved;
        I had thought it once was me.

You didn't need me, but I needed you;
    You stayed as long as you wanted to
        And didn't think twice about saying goodbye.
Goodbye, my love, goodbye;
    Now every night I cry on the pillow you left behind.
        Remembering you once were mine;
        You were mine.

Long Ago

Rain falling softly, misting in shadows;
    Cool breeze blowing, my hair drifting free.
Looking through teardrops I stare at those shadows;
    Those dark, dreary forms that bring back yesterday.

Wondering on why and wondering on how
    And beginning to ponder, "Did it happen at all?"
But like some cold winter dream the flash of the memories
    Reminds me of summers that passed long ago.

You left me wondering and asking and praying,
    "Why, oh God, why did you and I
    Have to leave our spring in the depths of the fall?"
So long, oh, so long ago…
    Why, oh why, did you have to leave and hurt me so?
      I can't let my dreams…go.

Another Sad Story

The people in my life, we change;
    Like the moon, like the night, like the times of long ago.
I waste away, hollow inside; my past, I try to deny.
    I remember, and I cry… Lord, don't you know how to cry?

Don't let me be alone with my memories.
    What could have been won't ever be,
      What is, I'm too blind to see;
And the path I travel runs barren,
    And a barren road's so lonely.

I'd like to stay to tell some stories
    And true ones make the best.
But I've got to go for if I stay

I know that all too well;
There'll be another sad story to tell…
There'll be another sad story to tell.

Foolish

Foolish talk, foolish deeds,
  Are all I can see when I look inside.
Fool's schemes, fool's dreams;
  They idle my life away.
    Tell me, why do I waste my time here today?

Foolish talk, foolish deeds;
  Follow all the time
These foolish thoughts, fool's dreams,
  That echo in my mind.
Tell me, please tell me,
  Won't someone please to tell me,
If there's even any meaning
  In those fool's thoughts I find.

Some say,
  It's only the fools who fall in love;
And others say
  That it's all because a case of fool's luck.
Well, I say
  It's the real fools who only go back for more;
Time after time love only leaves us
  Wondering what we come back for.

This time, next time,
　　Just like the time before;
　　　　All that we're left with
　　　　　　Are these fool's foolish dreams.

I, Revealed

I see myself walking slowly
　　Through the darkened caves of memories not experienced.
A dark wind, a heavy dew,
　　Falls upon my shoulders; myself…here.

I call out to the people around me;
　　A few hear me, treasures to be thankful for.
Deep inside grows a need
　　Ever blossoming, one inside of me.

Fruition of a dream; I cry at night.
　　No one hears, no one cares.
Lonely I walk, my soul shakes;
　　Give me peace, hold me tightly,
　　　　I'm so afraid.

Victims

We are all victims of emotion, of need.
　　Win a little, lose a little;
　　　　Appeal the verdict we plead, "We're only human."

Victims of time,
  Of love, of life;
Caught in the middle, tangled in the strife
  Of the needs to care, to touch,
    To feel.

Victims of emotion, victims of need;
  We beg to the world, still we plead
    For someone to understand and touch us inside;
Even for a moment,
  So that we can say that we've known
    How it feels not to have faced life...
      Completely alone.

Lonely Town

Loud resonant chords;
  Echoing through the empty corridors,
Along the paths
  Of a still and stately world.

Quietly growing softer,
  Yet lingering in my memory;
Persecuting,
  My hopes and dreams stand still.

Dear friends, I beg of you,
  Shun this place of utter despair.
It burns souls
  And cripples the heart and mind.

Damning in its eternal existence,
    I crave both to stay and leave;
Hopelessly lost,
    Wandering in my own realm.

Hear the dreary howl of a gale wind
    Blowing along foreboding avenues;
This is lonely town
    And in its center lies my heart.

Cry Alone

I want to cry, I'm so alone;
    My friends, my lovers, me…we cry so alone.
In our sorrow we stand so alone;
    Alone in our hearts, alone in our minds; cry souls.
Let a tear stain your heart and your soul feel empty,
    But let not a stifled sob choke your voice;
        That's being human.
So when you're lonely; in the dark, in your bed.
    Cry souls, cry alone.

My Friend Alone

The cold winter winds; biting skin, chilling bone.
    Tear-stained cheeks; those reminders of me and Alone.

Silent velvet dusk announcing the close of another day;
"Hello, old friend, Alone with me here, I bid you stay."

So many know you; with blank stares and lifeless eyes
They greet you. Smiles uncertain; all in disguise.

I'm tired, so tired of futile search; only you I find.
Visions rehearsed, and aged memories of feelings confined.

My Loneliness

I sit at my window
Watching the silent street below;
A couple passes hand in hand.
Hearing their laughter in the wind
I look inside my loneliness;
Too alone to care,
Too numbed to cry,
And wondering if my somewhen
Is really never in disguise.

I look about my silence
And I start to wonder,
If my heart could be as empty
As the life through which I live.
To the tune of the lonely ticking
Of the faceless clock on the wall,
I write this testimony
Of a man condemned
To the vanity of his loneliness.

I Can't Feel Nothing Inside

I can't say I'm lonely,
    Because the lonely have feelings;
And I can't say I've been hurt,
    Because to be hurt
        We need to have known how to love.

So I guess I'm just alone;
    Know nobody and care even less.
With no future and no past
    That's the way it must be,
        'Cause I just can't feel nothing inside.

So I'll say what I care to
    About the way I used to be;
'Cause being hurt
    Came in last winter's dream,
And now I've forgotten what feelings are made of
    And people just aren't what they seem.

So that's the way I'll take my chances;
    Maybe someone will see and care enough
        To wake my heart out of its sleep.
But until then I know that's the way it will be;
    I don't feel nothing inside…
        I just can't feel nothing inside.

Losers Know

Losers know; how to love,
    How to cry, how to say goodbye.
To feel alone, empty inside;
    To love and lose and never know why.

Losers know good things don't last;
    How to hide their hurt and remember the past.
They know how to watch, forget how to learn;
    Hide love inside, know how to yearn.

Losers know; yes, they know
    What it's like to begin and how it always ends;
Embrace how they've lived, and yet never win.
    Losers know.

Embraceless

For life is like a raging river and I am but a stone;
    Forgotten on the stream bed bottom, bereft of any home.
A witness in time, constant streams of people;
    I see all that I see.
Friends pass by, only a while they stay,
    In the end abandoned me.
Am I fated forever to live a life
    Without someone to call my own?

I

I laugh, but I do not feel joy;
　　I am concerned, but I do not shed a tear for you.
In the dark with my fears, I am frightened;
　　But comfort I do not seek.

I want someone to confide in, but I cannot;
　　For myself, I do not trust.
You are my friend
　　And I would give for you my life,
　　　　But I won't love you.
I seek for the fullness of being;
　　But in my heart rings hollow silence.

There is something inside
　　That I cannot let go
　　　　No matter how hard I try.
I had given it once
　　And it somehow returned;
　　　　To lose it for good I would die.

Myself, I fear to risk it again;
　　When I keep it
　　　　Inside I cry.
Until I'm ready to give one more time,
　　All I can do is get by;
　　　　I pray that my vigil is not in vain.

Finished

The ivory cold dagger has pierced my back;
    Its point has found my heart.
In my life I've never felt so finished,
    Not sure I even want to start...
        Living again.

Identity

Living on The Edge

Living on The Edge, looking all around me;
　　Trying to understand myself, wanting to believe.
But all I know is confusion;
　　Myself...what do I need?

In a life of mystery, memories pass me by.
　　Feelings drift around me, words only make me cry.
Oh, how I want to forget, but all I do is cry.
　　Can't the angels take me home? Oh, I feel so all alone.
　　　　Just leave me alone, so life can pass me by.

How do I believe when I cannot be?
　　How can I live when all hope fades,
　　　　When the shore runs from the sea?
Then the waves come singing, giving promise once again;
　　But like the sand before the wind trying to escape the sun,
　　　　Frightened and blinded; I run.
　　　　　　See me run.

Living on The Edge, looking all around me;
　　Trying to understand myself, wanting to believe.
But all I know is confusion, myself...
　　What do I need?

Living on The Edge, the lessons are forgotten;
　　Life, unforgiven.

All that we wait for will be in the end.
In a life that feels immortal, it's here that we're stricken;
Shattered and lonely, living on The Edge.
Here on The Edge.

One by One

I have loved,
    I have given,
        I have cried;
And for every minute passed by
    I have lost a little bit of myself.
I am confused because I just don't know
    If there's anything left…inside me.

What I need
    Is someone to share with me;
Fly with me,
    Cry with me,
        For just a little while.
Perhaps I'll see
    It hasn't left me;
        The power to feel.

But I'm afraid no one will listen
    Or care enough to see,
So the past is that of which I speak
    And not the dying me;
Who only watches the days roll past,

One by one by one.
For whom life only seems to last,
   Not living in the sun.

I need to see, I need to be,
   I need you;
      Even if it's only for just a little while.

The days roll past;
   I see the moon,
      I watch the sun.
One by one by one
   The days of my life pass me by;
      One by one by one.

To Be a Part

Wanting to share, wanting to be a part,
   Trying my best to fit in;
But I'm not quite right so I spend the night
   Wondering what it's like to win.

Everyone else has a part to fill
   And belongs here in some way.
That part I can't mime and so every time,
   Feel more alone every day.

Actor unknown, waiting for the part
   That will let them all know me;
But until that hour, my dreams grow sour
   And lonely shall I be.

Loner

Hold nobody,
    Have no one;
        Visions that there could be someone
           To need.

Friendships of convenience,
    Fantasies of love;
        Wishing, just wishing,
           To know the reality of
                Togetherness.

Reared in isolation,
    Living alone;
        Searching, just searching,
           For a place to call my own…
              Home.

To Find Our Place

We live, we go forward,
    We hope to do what's right.
For ourselves to continue,
    We seek to find our sight.

We explore and discover;
    Others' voices, they endeavor

To steer our every direction.
We hear their dreams;
    False ideals, misleading schemes,
        Sometimes even their confessions.

In choosing which paths we should pursue,
    Caution should be our guide;
Some would lead us to our dream's farthest ends,
    Others could take us for a ride;
        It's up to us to decide.

Some want for us to follow their leads,
    Blind us with their visions;
Others seek to be our guides,
    Not their ways but to seek our own;
        Not to cause in us self-division.

To discover the truths for our own lives,
    It's a better path to follow;
To learn to heed our voices within,
    Instead of the lies so easily swallowed
        From those whose desire is for us to submit.

The Unmasking

All my life I've yearned to feel free
    From my time filled with people
        Telling me who I should be.
Daily contentment, it eludes me;

People try to engage me with their lies and deceit.
　　Their false words that once ensnared me
　　　　Are now a useless tangle strewn about my feet.
Every moment I seek to expose the truth,
　　To put to the test what I hear;
The ones who care and those that don't,
　　Time to uncover the masks they wear;
　　　　Embrace the real, discard the fake.

How they talk, what they think,
　　Too easily hide a false face;
　　　　I want to reclaim my freedom,
　　　　　　I need to mark my own space.
The self-honesty of my inner heart;
　　Will guide my best way forward…
　　　　That which speaks to me from within
　　　　　　The depths of my soul.
In being true to myself
　　Therein lies the power;
　　　　That for the first time,
　　　　　　I will know what it means to be whole.

Dark Side

It seems to me I've come so far;
　　Yet I really don't know exactly who I are.
Is the day-to-day me the prophet who speaks true,
　　Or merely the shamster who hides the truth from you?
Don't come too close
　　For you may fall to what I fear;

You'll find I'm not who you think I am,
    And it may shatter your heart so open and dear
To discover the lie I live so well
    And see in its reflection…yourself.

The Stranger

I feel as a stranger to myself,
    Not knowing that which is me.
Is the life I live a truth or a lie?
    Inside I'm too blind to see.

The stranger lies within,
    I live my life in fear.
I know I can't trust him;
    So I sit alone, shed a tear,
        And grieve.

The stranger, he fears to touch
    Despite the need inside.
I want to care,
    To be loved so much;
But the stranger in his jealous pride
    Keeps everyone away;
        Fearing to hurt again.

The stranger lives within;
    Feeling sad, alone, and abused.
I bid you sincerely

Take care, my friend;
   For he would only seek to use you.

A special friend is what I need
   To quell that stranger within;
A friend to love,
   To stand, to be;
One who would want
   To help show me
The way,
   To learn someday…
How to love again
   And not be afraid to fall.

The Real Me

That for which is searched, that I can never seem to see;
   Always escaping, the real me.
With the world as my setting my hope lives on endlessly;
   Trying to find the real me.
All shared and given; I and my friends, us and we,
   The heart and love of the real me.
In my soul are there many, is it I entirely;
   Or him, her, you, and the real me?
Isolated to myself, or with you and he and she;
   Is it so or not?
I must find it to be…
   The real me.

Standing

I stand here alone;
    Not moving forward, not falling back.
My feelings stand alone;
    Not happy not sad, not white nor black.

I want to care, but I fear;
    I want to live, but my heart is somewhere
        And I cannot seem to find it.
It is hiding from my need inside,
    Afraid to hurt again;
Can there be a someone,
    Will there be a somewhen
        To make my dreams come true?

Here I stand alone;
    Not moving forward, not falling back.
My feelings stand alone;
    Not white, nor black.
I wait to learn to live again
    And keep my heart intact.

Led On

I don't know if I can love,
    I don't know what it is I'm thinking of;
Is what I need, the vision I see,
    Really the answer I seek?

There will come a day,
  When a choice will come to show the way
    To the path I dream someday will lead me home.
But when this day comes and the deed is done,
  Will I feel that this is where I've always wanted to be?

Is love what my heart needs to know to share,
  Or is it merely the dream that leads nowhere
    To keep me striving on;
Merely to be replaced with another
  After I have made it mine?

Sometimes I look at this world as a carnival game,
  A shining façade in the sun;
With my dreams the prizes that cannot be won
  And me, the fool, led on.
    Maybe my life is better lived alone.

Here and There

Here and there;
  Little reminders of times held dear,
Of those memories I fear;
  I know, they just keep coming back to me.

Here and there;
  Cloud shapes in the sky,
The reflections in my eye
  That tell of stories that passed long ago.

The failures of my past, the futures in my dreams;
    Keep me alive, help me survive,
Living in the hope
    That the learnings of my life will come through;
When my longings there meet my loneliness here
    And I won't feel alone anymore.

Here and there;
    The people I meet,
The denial of defeat;
    Believing that love will somehow arrive.

The people in my life
    Who I've loved, who I've wished the love of;
Pass by like mirages always on the horizon,
    But never before my eyes.
How I wish I could capture that dream
    Of someone to share love with forever;
        Faith is all I have in which to believe.

Here and there;
    Past and present I pass through.
Life; chasing your rainbow,
    Here in the moonglow,
        I, in my isolation…survive.

My Dream

In the shelter of despair, I sit
    And watch the darkened moon;

Feeling the touch of whispering madness,
    I sing this hollow tune.

The sorrow deep inside
    Has claimed my tortured soul;
The pain that's hid by silence
    Is for no one to behold.

The solace for my soul within
    Lies deep within my mind;
Though life denies that which I seek,
    Someday it will be mine.

You may wonder as to how I go on;
    I'll tell you so, my friend.
Faith is all I have for today
    And is all I have 'til the end...
        When I reach my dream, and it is mine.

One Little Corner

One little corner, careworn and bare;
    One little corner, there lies the lair
Of the time lost one alone, huddled to the side.
    Hidden from the world;
        No more spirit, no more pride
        Left to call his own.

One little corner, no one can see;

One little corner, fearing to be.
The small one faces life
    Without love, without pain;
Standing silent forward
    Looking onto the next day;
        Living so alone.

One little corner, careworn and bare;
    One little corner, you know that it's there
We hide that part of us inside, keeping it from all.
    Standing fast in isolation
        We hide behind our walls;
            Fearing to care.

I Believe

-1-
Here I stand;
    Crying, wandering in the rain.
I need to talk, I need to stay,
    I need to share my forgotten way;
        But I'm afraid the words you may not understand.

And so I write, to spill my heart in ink on page.
    I believe in right, someday it might
        Return to me, that which was lost in pain;
So that I may learn
    How to share my love again.

My dreams cannot stand still;
    We are blind to what is true.
I need a light to lead the way;
    Love, I wish it was you.
        Try to understand.

You fill my dreams, they fill my life,
    It's a special thing you do.
But now and then, alone again;
    I expect too much from you.
But when you come, dusk turns to sun,
    And my dreams like days renewed;
How very special you are for me,
    Am I the same for you?

Do you want me as I want you;
    Do you need me like I'd like you to?
Won't you comfort me like I do for you,
    Or is it only half a love we share?
Can you tell me, is it justice need
    Or a reflection of my human greed?
On folded knees I before you plead;
    Give me an answer, don't let it be no.

But as all things, affairs of heart
    Will end and yet another start.
On this rollercoaster ride I sail,
    I think I win and find I fail;
The whirlpool emotions send me 'round,
    My heart says love; I'm lost, I'm found.

Too much faith, too much trust, too much heart;
    I give into all the lies.
        In want for love my freedom flies.
I lose myself, I hurt, I pain;
    But yet I go right back again.
The circle, it turns 'round and 'round,
    It brings me up, it takes me down;
What madness in this life I've found!
    I only want it to STOP!!!

-3-

What I may show I may not feel; the scars I wear I know will heal.
    I reach out to find a helpful friend, I reach in to find myself again;
        I know what it all means to me.
I value my life, I value my love, I value myself;
    I know I can and will go on...I am.

I'm sorry that I lost your love,
    But you are still my friend;
Despite the fact that I got hurt
    I will still take the risk to love again.
Though the weight of life, it fell on me,
    I will not throw it away;
The pain of the past stays in my thoughts
    But I can still enjoy today, because I believe.

The music may end, the lyrics close,
    But the song will still live on.
What will come I may fear, but forward I go;
    Though impatient I still hold on.

I will live, I will grow, and I want you to know
   That someday for me it will be…because I believe.

I am Here

I am here, I am me;
   I'm not to be what you want me to be.
I am here, can you see; that to live on, I, myself,
   Must somehow strive to free my restless heart inside?

I am here, I live on; through laughter and tears,
   Souls come and hearts gone.
I am here, desire of me;
   Seeking wisdom, a life to be
Free of internal conflict; civil war.
   Yes, I confess, this is what I search for.

The Trap

Here I am, trapped in the center of my world.
   Not giving, but wanting to be given;
Self-pitying, demanding of compassion,
   But unwilling to give of myself.

My trap is my past;
   My chains, my refusal to let it go.
      My crime; my failure to grow.

I must learn to be myself; them, they are not me.
    This hollow shell I hide within obscures identity.
My sorrow for myself now must face an end.
    Life is that for which I reach, perhaps my heart will mend
        If I take the chance and live again.

Focus

In my problems, in my sorrows, in my memories of pain;
    I survive in desolation, a face without a name.
I sit and think on where I'm not, and where I long to be;
    I do not live my life in truth but in nonreality.

How can I be content with the spirit that is me
    If the dreams I hold inside cannot be set free?
I know I am impatient with where I am right now.
    I seek to be all that I can, all that which life allows;
        But I am unhappy.

I need to change my focus as to this life I live;
    I strive for dreams within my reach
But live my life as if
    They will never come true.
My future will come slowly and now I realize
    I need to focus on today for I find it now unwise…
        To wait for tomorrow to be content.

Witness I

Unseen Show

The door that will not open;
    The forest that becomes stilled when I appear
        Entices me to look inside.
But the secrets held within
    Are not for me to share;
        When I call, they hide.

My heart inside, which is denied;
    The wall is not for me alone.
This I know, this unseen show
    Is rarely played for anyone to see;
And is not as I have deeply feared,
    An expression of mistrust towards me.

Patient I will stay
    And my heart will hope and pray,
That someday this one I care for
    Will come to notice me
For what I have tried to be;
    A friend worthy of trust.

Dedication

Remain loyal to the faithless, believe in yourself;
    Shine your light, show you care,

Teach the laws of love.
Learn self-truth, strive to be free.
Dedicate yourself to the growth of others,
Help guide them to fully be;
Witness, in all things be true.

Witness

I have found you by your call for friendship;
I have heard your aching plea.
I hope you will take the time to listen;
I hope you can learn from me.

I will share with you what life has taught me
In my walk from day to day;
I hope you can grow from what I've learned,
From what I have to say.

I know you will think me wrong at times
Or perhaps not comprehend;
Just remember that I care for you,
True enough to be a friend.

I know that you may not agree
With all it is I say;
Open your heart, give careful thought
On what I offer today.
Listen to me…

Can It Be

Can a kingdom without border
    Stand fast upon the stone?
Can the wanderlust-worn traveler
    Ever find his home?
Can a newlywed, fresh in bed,
    Please his blushing bride?
Can a goalless man fit the master plan
    Or be taken for the ride?
Can a mellow tone for the all alone
    Ease the pain inside?
Can man through time without a sign
    Believe God will abide?

The Answer

I sing my song, a happy song,
    'Cause peace came through my door.
Alive inside, serenity guide;
    Not needing any more.

Faith the answer shows the way
    For inner peace in every day.
All you do for peace in you
    Is believe in God,
        And love,
            And you.

Reflection

For every negative thought,
    Think a positive thought;
For every positive thought,
    Think another positive thought.

Talking with a Friend

Times of joy, times of doubt,
    Times of love, times of fear;
In the rhythms of these emotions
    Live the colors of our souls,
        And we feel the need to express them, so
Here we are again;
    Together now just like back then,
Not afraid to let our hearts show
    The thoughts and feelings within;
        How special is the trust of a lifelong friend.

The time comes in the day
    When we all have our stories to share;
And talking with a friend
    There's no worry, there's no care
        About knowing the right words to say;
        A true friend will always understand.

As forward we boldly go,
    My friend, I want you to know,
That these paths which we've shared
    At times will lead us different ways.
Our lives, they carry on; the shadows, they grow long.
    Through the ever-faster years we live our days.

With each time we're rejoined, we get to share the joy
    In seeing lives and changes ever made.
Hearts and souls entwined,
    Years gone by and yet we find...
        Always we've remained the best of friends.

The roads I've walked along
    With a friend or all alone
        Have led me through these lessons learned anew.
Understand them, and all that you say you've been giving away
    Someday will come back to you.

Keep solitude, and your friendships will be full;
    Know loneliness, and your love can spread to all.
If you feel lost, know that someday you'll be whole,
    Self-truth and honesty are worthy of trust;
        Our sure and steady guides.
And true friends,
    They'll always be there to help us on our way.

So in talking to you, my friend,
    Years passed and now again; I want you to know that
        My deepest feelings for you will ever stay the same.
If you see what I'm trying to say,

Take heart and take hold of your life today,
Know this much is true;
    Just how much it is that I still love you.

Peace

First morning light;
    The lily-white mist rising with the dawn.
Sparkling reflections
    Mark the passing of Mother Nature's wand.

Sitting here on the mountainside,
    Presiding on freedom's domain;
Feeling the thrill in the beauty
    Of being at peace again.

I love the morning when time passes by
    And no one cares that it does.
To some it would seem a wasted day;
    But for finding a secret long forgotten…

Peace to ease the mind
    And to content the troubled soul,
Makes it so much more the thrill
    Of sitting at The Edge, rediscovering oneself,
And feeling the breathtaking joy in the simple self-realization
    Of the God-given right to be alive.

Shine

There's magic in people who shine.
  It makes me happy to shine
    And to be around those who shine.
Their magic and my magic, may it shine as one.
  Our paths cross, together we shine
    And then part.

Somewhere, somewhen; we who shine the brightest,
  Come a day when we may
    Rejoin to shine again.
But even if we don't, our magic will still shine on
  To touch all those around us
    Forever.

Legacy

My song is sung slowly for you to hear;
  Come closer now for there is nothing to fear.
    Take my hand, I will draw you near
      To witness my dream.
I am like the sea, deep and wide;
  Echoes of my heart flow with the tide.
    I welcome you to look inside;
      Share my dream.

Every soul has a place to belong;
  In each of us there lives a song.

Every heart can learn to be strong,
            Strong enough to care.
                That is my dream.

My time with you has come and gone;
        The music played, the painting drawn,
            The shadows grown long.
I have given myself to you
        In the sharing of my dream.
Remember what you have heard,
        Remember what you have seen
                Of this gift of life we pass on;
                    Pass it on.

Growth

Acceptance

We hear words of wisdom, tales of trials,
    Songs and stories;
Others all around us telling of how they came to be,
    Trying to convince us to see the world as they see it.

On The Edge,
    We are blinded by the shadows of memories;
        Lost in our worlds within.
We struggle to understand our pasts,
    To learn about what we can be;
        To accept that which we are.
Growth in self takes time,
    And learning comes in the experiences that life has to offer
        And our appreciation of them.

If we accept others into our lives
    And offer ours in theirs to share;
        I think...we can grow.

Steps

I grit my teeth, forward I go
    Into a future I do not know.

I fear this future because of my past;
    Each step I take seems just like the last.

My hopes, my dreams, deep they run;
    Sometimes I wonder, will they ever come?
My future I face, for right or for wrong;
    Though my steps seem uncertain, my waiting too long…
        I know I must go on.

The Gift

Encased in a soundless room;
    Groping in the darkness
        For someone, anyone.
            I ask you, give me me.
Groping, my senses dimmed,
    My soul obscured;
        Let me give of myself.
            This my plea, give me me.
But no! The curtains have closed,
    The last chord struck;
        Descending, sunset.
            Can it ever be for me to be me?
A prism before my eyes,
    Many facets reaching out;
        My friends will not desert me.
            They can see, I am me.

The Best People

Self-forgiveness leads to freedom;
    Compassion is a gift to all.
Balance within moves us forward,
    Catches us when we fall.

Judgment ever ensnares the soul;
    Inside, there's never peace.
The quest for perfection is a lie to ourselves,
    We never get release.

To find a better way for our lives
    We need to free our hearts and minds;
Self-blame only serves to hold us back,
    Honesty and truth are what we need to find...
        To grow into the best people that we can be.

Dreamer

Caught up in my own foolish ambitions;
    I live on.
Uttering meaningful words that fall on deaf ears;
    I sing on.
Trying to fulfill goals that lead to nonexistent ends;
    I strive on.
Passing by me, people cannot help
    But to turn their faces and laugh;
I hear them,
    I dream on.

Comes a Time

I see a lonely star through the window
    And the night whispers hello.
Comes a time in the life of every man
    When he wonders where to go;
What to do, who to be,
    How to let those restless feelings inside
        Out to the world so that he will know;
That there comes a time of being,
    Believing in the truth unspoke.
Wondering, hoping, and dreaming,
    That there will come a time
        In speaking the truth of his heart,
His song will be heard
    And he will be fulfilled;
Having found the one in soul
    To be with forever.
For every man there comes a time,
    And I only wait for me.

Lonely Nights

Listen to the lonely nights,
    Hear the echoes call;
As the stars shine down so bright and cold
    And the shadows on the wall
Remind you where you should have been

And where you're going to,
And the faces you've seen in your dreams
    Keep coming back to you.

Now boy, you say you've had your chance
    But let it slip right by;
The one-time dream that was none else,
    Captured by the sky.
Now you're still wondering how it ended,
    You're crying out your nights;
And wondering what you're going to do
    And where to set your sights.

Now listen closely to my story
    And try to understand,
Am I a boy so worldly lost
    Or merely half a man?
I like to hide behind my friends;
    I admit it so, it's true.
But why I run so fast from love,
    Am I so scared of you?

I really don't know what to think;
    It's very hard to say.
I seldom seem to want or know
    Or care about today.
Tomorrow holds the nightmares
    And the past the elder dreams;
A pleasant way to fool myself
    All is as hopeless as it seems.

Lonely nights are the only way
　　A man can be a man,
As day and night dreams shuffle by
　　And blow like desert sand.
Can the present ever give you peace
　　And the future never end?
And hope, like time, continues on;
　　And after now, there's always then.

Reflections on Love

Expect too much, give too little;
　　Or yet, to love and be taken.
Nay, the many faces of love;
　　Be it as cruel as it is warm.

Yet hate is as love, unlike yet like
　　The fine line twixt pain and ecstasy;
　　　　'Tis known no better than within oneself.

If one has wronged, forgive;
　　Slighted, welcome and take reassurance.
　　　　Denial of oneself, teach;
　　　　　　Yet once again, forgive.

Still always; always, always ever, love.
　　Despite any hurt;
　　　　Shine…Love.

My Hope

Though I know it inside as truth;
    Sometimes it is difficult for me to believe
    That there is someone out there
    Who wants and needs me
    As desperately as I want and need them.

Two Faces

Looking inside myself,
    Two faces I see;
        One is for you, one is for me.

I step, I run,
    Into...through the world.
Outside, I am bold.
    Inside, my blood is curled;
My fear so cold
    At the thought of talking to you.

And yet, at the sound of your name;
    My defenses crumble,
        My heart sets aflame.
I'm not the same;
    What's my name?

Yes, I Care

I'd like to make you promises
    So you'd be sure that I'd be there.
Oh, if I could give you my words, my love;
    Oh, if I might know I would care.

Long ago, there was a time when I was not afraid;
    Promises to pass and ever last
        That always, every day,
I'd be there to care for you if ever you should fall;
    To let you know someone loved you
        And would answer your every call.

But when the trust held was broken
    And my feelings cast aside
By the one I once held dear;
    Well…something died inside.

Now here comes the new day dawning
    With you and your love on the rise.
Oh, if only I could return what you promise,
    Oh, if only our words aren't lies;
        If only I could know and let myself care.

But if you've got the patience,
    Stay with me 'cause I know
That my heart inside might let me love again;
    Oh, it might let me be there to care for you.
And so for you this much I'll promise,

Call me and I'll be there.
And this one thing I can give you, my love;
My tears show…yes, I care.

Silence of a Moment

In the silence of a moment, ideas can be realized
That an eternity of words could never fulfill;
Thoughts you have never found the courage to say
Can be known, in the silence of a moment.
You can know and overcome the feelings
That have for so long kept your heart in darkness,
Find your inner self and the strength
To make your deepest dreams come true,
Discover that long-searched-for peace within yourself,
And learn the truest meanings of the word love…
All in the silence of a moment.

Namaste

Eyes touch, hands touch, we understand;
To know each other this much
Is better than
Anything before.
I know you, you know me, only as a friend;
In the rain we part our ways,
But now I know I can…
Share again.

Listening

My days pass by, I stand on square one.
　　My desire is high, but what must be done?
　　　　I must decide.
I think back to where I started,
　　To where we had begun;
How did we grow and come to know
　　Our togetherness as one?

Memories come into passing
　　Of how I came to care.
I recall the nights we talked;
　　Remember the way we shared.

A special night, a special friend;
　　How close we were, we touched.
I heard you talk of love, of dreams,
　　Of loneliness and such.

Listening was the way I grew
　　To be there for a friend;
A witness I see is what I must be
　　To learn to grow again…
　　　　I choose to grow again.

Unsure

I remind myself to be at peace;
　　Few use words like I do.

To simply say in a simple way,
　　Those three words "I love you."
Some are unsure to share, to hug;
　　I know, I understand.
But what I see in their eyes
　　Tells the truth in their hearts,
Not every friend can show what I can;
　　That which is there inside.

Freedom

My life flies by before my eyes;
　　Learning, yearning, aching to feel free.
Wanting, needing to be me;
　　Who do I think I am?

Others, what they've wanted of me, from me;
　　Expectations at my door.
For me, these now are vacant;
　　I'm now content, now secure.

It's true, this is a grand thing
　　No matter what they think.
Me, I know who I am now, exactly as intended…
　　Life is but a blink.

Too short lived to be unhappy,
　　Now I rest assured.
I know myself—
　　Who I am, what to be;
　　　　Within myself, I've found my own cure.

Freedom, it is a good thing;
   It's ours, just waiting to be found.
In that moment we discover
   We don't need to be bound
      By what and who it is that others think we should be.

Growing

Have you ever felt like growing?

No matter how much you know
   Or how much you think you know,
There's always room to learn;
   To expand, to seek your farthest horizons,
Bound beyond the known limits
   You have placed before yourself.

Have you ever felt like growing?

In discovering the teacher within
   And sharing yourself with others
      In the forms of ideas and thoughts,
You can grow and live and love,
   Reveling in the growth of one another;
Finding the newness within you,
   Learning to be someone more
      Than just yourself.

Have you ever felt like growing?

Witness II

Trust

Trust in small secrets leads to rapport;
    Trust in rapport leads to intimacy.
Trust in intimacy leads to true friendship;
    Trust in true friendship leads to love.

Coupling

Hearts filled with love, couples walk hand in hand
    On the edge of a star beam;
As enchanted melodies play,
    And the words of minstrels reach up onto the heights
        Of serene angel-trimmed peaks.
They embrace tightly in each other's arms
    As if they could hold forever;
        Their lips quivering, quenching need.
On rainbow paths their existence,
    With the passing of the seasons
        Endures throughout the thread of time.
Surrounded in comforting darkness,
    In fairytale castles they exist;
        Finding security in the touch of
            Their bodies entwining warmth.
Falling into fragrant blossoms

They run to the edge of their dreams,
And together fall into one.

Distance

In love with each other, two become one.
Two, learn to share; in love, learn to care.
With growth comes test, comes trial;
Can love bend in the wind and not break?
In moments of such discord, sometimes deaf ears are turned,
And the one becomes two again.

Do not assume love
Conquers all only in its spirit.
The two must know in their strife lest they be lost forever,
Each the other's thoughts.
If such is not;
Love fades, distance grows.

As humans, we are weak and assume too much.
Words, thoughts, feelings…
Mean little if left to themselves;
They must be shared.

Love can be blind; if not seen, if not heard,
If not shared, if not touched.
Take heed, my friend;
Do not let your pride allow your love to die.

Treasure

Treasure the witness of the sudden moment
   When the quiet soul emerges;
Sometimes needing to share a part
   Of a private and unknown existence,
Giving a glimpse of concealed heart.
   Treasure the moment.

Your Way

You tell me, my friend, with a tear in your eye,
   That the love you held once is gone;
And the ones you hold close have no time to share
   And your nights seem so sad and alone.

Oh, my friend, don't despair,
   There's no worry, there's no care;
I'll be here to comfort you
   If ever you should call.
And the love you feel you need
   Will be there for you to see;
If only you would look my way,
   There's a friend who'll stand beside you here today.

Now you tell me, my friend,
   All the love has come and gone.
Why do the ones we care for

Touch us and say goodbye?
Now I'll tell you, my friend,
    There are ways things have to be;
Now listen very closely,
    I'll tell you what I've seen.

A friend, that's the time
    Two choose to share together.
The sad thing is, they can't be held,
    It may only last a while.
You know for friends there comes a day
    When you'll go your separate ways,
        And your final touch will hide a tearful smile.
But I want you to remember,
    You can hold them close if you try.
Though you know you can't be together,
    There's no need to say goodbye;
        A true friend will never leave you alone.

As the sun touches the sky,
    These times will pass you by;
The hurt inside will pass at last,
    You'll give it one more try.
There's a promise in your life,
    You will find a love to stay;
Someone to fill your empty heart
    And share your special way.

But until the moment of your dream,
    The dawning of that day;
Live as full as you can,

Lend a helping hand,
    Find a friend to share your way…
      And you'll never be alone.

After the Fall

-1-
The all we shared, my love,
    Lies, oh, so far away.
The time we tried to save,
    My life, it seems to slip away.
Oh, I love you more than I can say;
    Oh, I wanted you, I needed you,
And then I heard you say…
    Goodbye.

My world, it's falling apart.
    I need to learn, to want, to say;
To find out how to start to know
    To keep you from turning away.
Oh, my love; I cry, I cry,
    I cry today.

No, I can't survive without you,
    Without you here today;
Without you here close at my side,
    I can't seem to find my way.

I pray to God my life to take,

For your return I cannot wait;
My soul to keep should I not wake,
    I fall asleep, is it too late?
        I fall asleep, I fall asleep; I weep.

Awakened out of sleep,
    Who has rescued me?
I want to hear, I want to know,
    Why simply did you not let me go?
        I need to know.

-2-

My friend, listen carefully;
    These words you need to hear.
Do you not know that to care for yourself
    You must face life without fear?
And forward you must go,
    Despite all the blows it has made you bear.

You are a person of value,
    A center of life for which you care.
The one you once had treasured,
    The one with whom you shared;
Was a gift, freely given,
    And was taken away
Because she chose to do
    What she thought was best for herself.

Now this time in through your passing,
    Bears scars which may never seem to heal.
Take heart, my friend,

Life sees it time and again;
Through the frustration,
    The hurt, the pain…we survive.

-3-
If we are secure in ourselves,
    If we can take pride in who we are,
        In what we can grow to be;
And not look to others to live our lives,
    To depend on them, entirely…
        We can recover from any fall.

That is not to say
    Do not take the risk to share;
        For it is in others that we can be made complete.
Live life, share love,
    For all it can give, for all you can give…
        Be.

People Can Change

There're no shadows to fall on top of you
    When you fly high above the clouds;
And no need to build a wall around you
    If you surround yourself with crowds.
And as long as you say no
    To the feelings deep down inside;
There'll be no friends, no loves, nobody,
    To find the you that died…when she went away.

And so, my friend, look around you,
    There's always room for change.
In your life, your joys and sorrows
    Have got you feeling past your age;
You've got the future in which to believe
    That someday she'll come back and never leave.

'Cause she'll know that you've been changed,
    Though perfect you won't be;
And look within her mirror, herself,
    And come to finally see
That perfection is a gift unknown,
    Despite what the prophets cry;
And love means learning to grow together,
    To never say no and always try
        To give more than you feel you can.

Remember, people can always change
    If they know someone's got the love to give;
And faith is the word that will lead the way
    When you know that to love is to live.

Loyalty and Friendship

For You, My Friend

I sing for all you dreamers;
 A beacon in the darkest night.
I try to give your all to you,
 Those hopes for which you have the right.
But tears were all I gave to you.
 Yes, my friend, that's all I could do;
  I'm sorry, my friend, that's all I could do.
If I could have a single wish
 I know right now what I would do;
  I'd seek out all the lonely hearts
   And make their dreams of love come true.

I listen to the people;
 The opening of the lonely hearts.
They shower me with all their fears,
 I give them comfort and we part.
But the dreams are not mine to give.
 You ask, my friend, for what we live;
  The future, my friend, is for what we live.
If I could have a single wish
 I know right now what I would do;
  I'd seek out all the lonely hearts
   And make their dreams of love come true.

To the side I sit watching

The present fall from futile past;
I see dreams come and see dreams go,
    Why do they never seem to last?
Cry for help and I'll hear your call.
    For you, my friend, I'll give my all;
        Let me help, my friend, you can have my all.
If I could have a single wish
    I know right now what I would do;
        I'd seek out all the lonely hearts
            And make their dreams of love come true.

Allegiance

Smile upon the allegiance
    Of a heart, a mind, a soul;
        Do with it what you will.
Appreciate, ignore,
    Fulfill, love,
        Return…
It does not matter what you do with it;
    Simply let it be known
        That it is felt…here.

Real

I am me, you are you;
    I thank you for your love so true.

You are you, I am me;
    In my eyes you are truly free
To be exactly that which you are.
    Together we can be completely…real.

Our bonds are all accepting;
    No shadows to ever hide.
We speak softly to each other
    In love from deep inside.
Together all we've shared,
    Never are we alone;
Entwining our emotions,
    Confiding all we've known;
        Together we are free to be…real.

In your eyes I can be fully me.
    My heart's shelter you'll ever be;
        My trust and thanks are yours to call your own.
In my eyes, you are you;
    Know every day your freedom to
        Be also, always…real.

Friendship

I have led a life so young, and yet so rich.
    I have touched the closeness of friendship;
    not once, but many times. I take pleasure
    in the security of knowing one of life's
    greatest comforts; I am loved.

A true sharing friendship is surely one of the
    greatest gifts that the world has to offer.

I Thank You

I thank you for accepting me as I am,
    I thank you for being a friend;
I thank you for being on the path which I tread,
    For standing with me to the end.

I thank you for wanting to know me;
    I thank you for the courage you've shown.
In you I've found a someone who cares,
    With you my heart's found a home.

I thank you for the peace you bring,
    For your honesty so true.
I thank you for your love for me
    And I thank God for you.

Giving Myself

Time and time again
    You live in my thoughts, my friend.
Though you may be many miles or only seconds away;
    I still feel you close to me.

To you I give myself for I can think of nothing else;

    A more precious gift to you there could never hope to be.

Myself, my gift to you, is a wonder you will know

    For all the love you've shown;

        And all I ask is share it now with me.

Friend is a word often misused;

    For some, a memory of feelings abused.

        I, myself, would rather die first than to see you hurt that way.

A loving friend is special to me,

    And deep inside is all I want to be…for you.

When I live those full and deep moments

    Of sharing and caring inside for someone I hold dear

        And I feel that they truly care for me,

Then is the time I agree to call another my friend;

    And they have the gift of me.

When I desire to give to a friend,

    The selfishness and human greed inside

Like the autumn's fallen leaves,

    Simply die and blow away.

What remains is a bare and simple solitude

    Open to the sight of all,

Waiting for the embrace of the new day

    And the warming touch of a friend.

Though you may not understand,

    Walk beside me, take my hand;

Look deep inside my soul and see the peace within

    That with your presence you bring to me.

I give to you myself, I give to you my trust;
   Because I know you inside as I've known you times before.
With your friendship, with your being,
   I find my own true worth;
      I embrace the love I feel for you.
And in the sharing of our friendship,
   I find me.

Brothers

Brothers part, go separate ways;
   Live out their lives, go through the days
      Until they can be together again.

When I have my brother close to me,
   He gives me strength, helps me get by;
      And lends a shoulder when I have to cry.
He shows me love, makes me feel at home;
   And stays so close when I feel so alone.

That's the way it was;
   That's how brothers should be.
I will always remember you and what it means to me
   To have you as my brother;
      My friend.

Goodbyes and Memories

Parting Thoughts

Look into the crystal-cold gray depths of the mirror that is you;
    Live every one of the thousand eternal moments that is you.
Your humility is the cornerstone of your ability to draw those to you
    Who will make your most loyal and trusted friends,
        Because they will see more in you than you see in yourself.
Remember that it is in listening to others that you learn;
    And though you don't realize it,
        There is so much of you, you can teach.
You let others know you not for who you are,
    But for that which you represent;
        You represent that which you believe.
Beloved, God has given me sight,
    And I can see that some of your highest beliefs are life and love.
Live out those ideals no matter what the cost
    And you can find the great peace that is within yourself;
And the ends to which your dreams ever reach
    Will be only a moment away, and will live forever…
        If truly in your heart you so desire.

First Love

Return to my love of youth;
    Young love, first love, where are you now?

Time passed ago, you taught me to grow;
　　Taught me to care, let me know
　　　　How to share myself with you.

First love, fine love; my memories of you,
　　Are filled with thoughts of how we grew
　　　　To give ourselves as one.

Young love, first love, where are you now?
　　I'm filled with wishes of, someday, somehow,
　　　　To find another like you.

Past Departing

The past is gone, lived once in time,
　　Yet how I miss the days.
Memories weep, the good times keep,
　　The bad times throw away.

Where are you, my friend?
　　I loved you so, do you ever think of me?
It's you I miss, my fondest wish
　　Is that you could really see
　　　　The me, I never showed to you.

Did you love me? It doesn't matter,
　　'Cause in some future day,
Even the memories that I hold dear
　　Some dusk will slip away.

You have the pictures, I have the poems;
　　In my heart, the story.
And the song—deep, you left in my heart,
　　Will not die forgotten, slowly.

Reminisce

Memories fade
　　Like ocean waves,
　　　　Nestling in the foam;
Revering thoughts
　　Of long ago
　　　　Where times content have roamed.
Comforts thought
　　And memories fraught
　　　　With ancient, spindled gold;
Think of the hearts lost,
　　Loved behind…
　　　　Shining in the cold.

You Let Me Love You

You let me love you;
　　With my words, my heart, my feelings, you let me touch you.
You give my heart wings, on a zephyr it floats above;
　　　Though you won't be mine you're a friend through time
　　　　And will ever have my love.

You gave me your love;
　　With your words, your heart, your feelings,
　　　　Strengthened me to go on.
Though our time was short, I still recall that quiet night;
　　When I learned all the more
Of what it is we live for;
　　To love all we can is what's right.

You let me love you;
　　With my words, my heart, my feelings,
　　　　You let me touch you.
You give my heart wings, on a zephyr it floats above;
　　Though you can't be mine, you're my friend through time
　　　　Who I will always, ever love.

Memories

Fond memories make us warm inside;
　　Free us, make us whole.
Friends and loves are the treasures that fill
　　The hollows of our souls.
Our thoughts, they dwell; our hearts, they swell;
　　Endear the times we've touched;
Reflections of the memories shared
　　That mean so much to us.
Memories mirror, bright and clear,
　　The seasons left behind;
Like polished glass, they shine on as
　　Our treasures for all time.

A Secret Box

A winter night;
    A letter to write,
        To say the precious things I want to say.
Shining light,
    Secret delight;
        Your voice can change my darkness into day.

I'm thinking of
    Memories beloved;
        The special times I've spent as one with you.
Loving, caring,
    Giving, sharing;
        I thank you for the touching things you do.

Your heart so deep;
    I want to keep
        Alive the thoughts and words we've shared of past.
Despite my fears,
    It's through the years
        Our brotherhood of soul and hope will last.

Open for me your secret box;
    Tell me of the stories that have been.
Let me draw to keep
    From your well so deep;
        Show me your discoveries again.

Your spirit of hope,
    It helps me to cope
        With each new day as it begins.
The key that unlocks
    Your secret box
        Is a treasure I hold within.
I know and love you;
    You're my friend.

The Call

The Call

The emotional experiences we go through
    All share a common thread.
We learn by what it is we do;
    All through our lives we're led
        To face ourselves.

Too many times these experiences seen
    Can lead us to despair.
Too often what we want and need
    Is someone who can share,
        Someone to care…and there's no one there.
I find comfort in the knowledge
    That I am not alone.
There lies the chasm I seek to bridge,
    My need, to make it known;
        To pass it along to others.

On The Edge the paths we follow
    Are common to us all;
My gift to you is to show myself,
    To have you join my Call.
I seek to see all self-beloved,
    Our wars within to cease;
That we may learn to live our lives
    Content, in inner peace.

Self-Honesty

Dishonesty with self, secrets from self.
      Secrets from self, nonacceptance of self.
Nonacceptance of self, mistrust of self.
      Mistrust of self, dislike of self.

Escapism

What makes people hurt so easy?
      Really, I don't know.
Is life to be born to never be lived;
      Is it really such a dirty rotten show?
What makes people need to escape from themselves,
      Are they all so ugly inside?
They treat themselves like the dirt on the ground,
      As if they've already died;
And are no more than a memory…
      Fleeting, passed away;
            Already forgotten.

What makes people think they can run from themselves;
      Why do they even try?
The farther they run, the clearer they see
      This life as a phony lie.
What makes people hurt so easy,
      Why don't they learn to like what they see?
There's a lot of good inside

That can be loved, can be shared;
If only we could all learn to be
More honest with ourselves.

It's so easy to run, to hide, to be lost,
Anywhere but where we are;
It's much harder to learn, to live, to dare,
To face that what we are.
Pain lost in pain, a life lived in vain,
Its fullness, never to be seen;
What makes people run, I don't understand,
When there is so much for them to be?

Holding Back

What we desire is oneness, not to be alone;
A heart to love, a touch to share, someone to be our home.
Somewhere, nowhere; how hard it is to believe.
Living in isolation, it's so easy to deceive…ourselves.

Closed doors cannot be entered, how is it shall we go?
We hope for someone to say yes; too often it is no.
How hard it is to join with others, inside so insecure;
To overcome what holds us back, afraid we are of tears.

But still we recognize as truth,
Our paths must cross, this much we know;
If we stay unseen, our dreams can't be.
We, afraid to let go.

The challenge now before us; to be more than today.
No longer must we hold it back, nor stand in our own way,
If we are to make the most of our lives.

Honest Feelings

I guess this old world
Wasn't made for honest feelings.
(Fear)

Show a little, and people turn their backs
And just walk away.
(For themselves)

So I'll just have to keep all those honest feelings
Locked down deep inside.
(Hidden away)

I may not be able to show people all that I feel,
But at least they'll be around.
(I wait to share love)

I'll be crying, for every lost word and feeling;
Losing a heart, living a lie.
(With them someday)

Draw the Line

To be me, living this life the way I want it to be;
Giving my affection is what sets me free
And now they're trying to take it away,
Trying to tell me not to love today.
Where do they think they can draw the line...around me?

The walls, the stark blue-gray granite faces they hide behind;
Just because that's the way they live, they think it should be mine.
The smiles and the empty words they say come from their hearts
Ring untrue.

If they would listen to me,
I could help them learn to start to feel;
To draw the line that refuses to yield
To that stubborn cold gray granite within
And learn to accept everyone as they are.

This is where I draw the line
And all are welcome inside,
And I pity those who refuse to grow;
Who would rather close their hearts and die.

For them, I draw the line that leads to my door
And I burn my candle bright;
For a day may come when they'll finally listen
And learn to understand just how right...
Is everyone's need for love.

Desert in My Mind

The desert in my mind lies far across the sea.
　I see an orphan child sitting there, he looks a lot like me.
There's sand in his clothes, tears in his eyes, he's staring at the sun;
　Our thoughts, our dreams, join into streams, "I wish my life was done."

My soul, it finds this body a stranger, a captive bird constrained,
　My tattered wings, a will of anger, frustrated and dismayed;
　　I strive to be free.
The spirit that is me yearns to fly away;
　Far to the sea, far to the sky, far from this desert today.
But day to day I live in shadow, in steel cold chains unkind;
　Alone within myself I stay, a prisoner within my mind.

My time, it seems a circle; a nowhere–somewhere-nowhere life.
　From day to day I tread my way, but nothing's turned out right.
The things I touch turn to ashes; the ones I love blow away…
　So of what use then is this life I lead?
　　Alone I believe is the place to be;
　　　I have come to this desert to stay.

Sitting here alone I feel the darkness closing in.
　The breeze, it starts to blow so hard; a crashing, galing wind.
The raindrops start to fall to mingle with my tears;
　Thunder and lightning join as one, in concert rage my fears.

But as quickly as they come, they die; I recall the life I live.
　Has my rage…has my life served a purpose? I believe they never did.
The storm, it now has passed into the failing light.
　Cold and wet I grieve, I sleep, away the fallen night.

The next day dawns, clear and strong, I say farewell to the night.
I open my eyes and look to see a truly amazing sight.
I watch a simple flower standing in the sand;
A simple delight, breathing life, into this desert land.

I felt it was a gift to me, this beauty undefiled.
It seemed to know my presence; it bloomed a colored smile.
The day was hot, the flower could not, long in the sun survive.
I watched it fold upon itself; it shed a tear and died.

I sit and think of the flower and of the courage it had shown;
To live a life so brief, so dear, in a hostile desert home.
I realized then that somehow, although I don't know why,
The flower knew its time was short before it had to die.

But with its life, its presence, in the moments it was there;
It spread its hope, its beauty, around it. It showed that it could care.
Although its time was short and it knew that deep inside;
It lived a life so full of glory, so bountiful in pride.

And then I took a look inside at where my heart has been;
And wondered why I chose to die, not seeing life a friend.
I chose to see my spirit as a song not made to sing;
Too easily hurt and broken, a simple fragile thing.

But a humble flower sang its song, it spoke out loud to me.
It showed me how to live my life and all that it could be.
Through its lowly wisdom, it taught me how to share;
Through its passing quietly, I learned then how to care.

So through my time the sun will shine, the beauty of the day,
Will give to me, will set me free to live life as I may.
And my soul's flight can be a light for others now to see;
I can show them now,
I can teach them how
To fly above the sea.
To live,
To care,
To love,
To be.

Wings

Let your heart be free as a bird in flight.
Imagine what it is like to stretch your wings and soar; to fly
Above all of the burdens and troubles this world has to offer.

Experience the feeling of peace,
The solitude of being one with Earth and sky;
Flying on the wings of love, letting yourself be free
To share as one within the world.
Your heart, the sea, the sky, the stars;
Experience the harmony of the world around you.

Stretch your wings, share your heart, let yourself go.
Reach out into the world around you and make it one within;
Let it burst forth like a rising sun.
Shout it out from deep inside;
Let it shine bright to touch and embrace all those around you.
Fly...on the wings of the wind; on the wings of love.

Caring

Life is so much brighter when lived under the sun.
A soul feels so much lighter reaching out to someone,
Loving someone; alive!
The light inside, in giving, in sharing,
Lives and grows; in loving, in caring for others.
It takes courage to share; not everyone wants to give.
Sometimes when we open our hearts,
Be an example, show how we live;
We are denied and the hurt inside
Becomes merely another burden to bear.
But be content, we have dared to touch another person inside;
We have tried.
Life is so much brighter when we live under the sun.
Our souls feel so much lighter when we touch someone,
Love someone; we feel alive!

Who Do You?

Who do you like to talk to?
People who are busy talking about themselves and not taking
care about how they sound to others, or people who actually
listen to you and care about what you have to say?

Who do you choose to truly listen to?
People who only try to get you to do what they want just for
their benefit or advantage, or people who want the best possible
outcomes for both of you?

Who do you give your trust to more?

> People who look out only for themselves, or people
> who have a genuine interest and concern for the happiness
> and well-being of the others they encounter in their lives?

Who do you like to spend your time with more?

> People who negatively try to put other people down and who
> have little kind to say about yourself and others, or those who
> have a self-assured and positive outlook on life and who are
> a pleasure to have as companions?

Who do you feel drawn to care about more?

> People whose only desire is for you to cater to their expectations,
> or those who take an active interest in and have compassion for
> both you and others?

Love your children, love your parents,
> Love your spouses, love your friends,
> > In all the right ways;
Any they will want to talk with you,
> Listen to you, trust you, be with you,
> > And love you in return.

Retrospect

Soul People

Lovers and true friends.
    There seems to be an obvious difference;
        Is it truly so?

A couple holds hands together.
    The radiance of their dreams
        In pounding surf; realization of self.

People; share a prayer
    Of peace, of joy, of love.
        Discover one another on the shores of the universe.

A chant to the stars;
    The gentle passing of a lover's last song
        As the world listens in awe.

Behold those who share,
    They are the chosen;
        Their love drifts deeply in the well of eternal oneness.

Explain the soul of the moon;
    The heart of a lofty mountain.
        Tell what a lover is, define a friend.

Fulfillment

Find yourself;
Uplift your heart, and show your
Love for your
Friends. Take an
Interest in people; live
Life and
Listen to them. Share their
Moods, their thoughts, their dreams.
Endeavor to be more than just yourself.
Never say no, and
Teach others by your example.

Sharing

Sharing a thought;
    A simple letter, a quiet melody,
        Subtly giving oneself.

Ambitions realized,
    Stories of a dreamer;
        Watch and listen and take heart.

Happy memories;
    Sorrowful, soulful songs.
        The family legend, may it never die.

Watch the watcher,
  Impressions given;
    Lovers and friends, know their examples.

Find yourself in others everywhere;
  Let your heart flow
    Out to those you love.

Never Say No

Never say no to listen; never say no to talk.
  Always say yes to show you care,
To share with others your walk.
  Witness, be true.

Someday

On some days in their lives, all feel lost;
  Someday, the lost will be found.
Yesterday I was lost;
  Tomorrow, come some day, I will be found.
    Where am I today?

Fear

'Tis not a question of not caring;
  Simply, it is the fear of what might happen

If we allow ourselves to care too much.
Question: is the joy of love enough to recompense
The hurt that can easily enough follow?

Believe

Believe in yourself
And your ability to love.
Believe in others;
They believe, too.
Try to remember
That you're not alone;
Try to remember
That someone loves you.
Believe…

Integrity

Honesty, or the lack thereof,
Is who a person is.
Morality, or the lack thereof,
Is what a person does.
Respect, or the lack thereof,
Is what a person gives.
Compassion, or the lack thereof,
Defines how well a person loves.

It is through these by which
   Others will recall us.
How fondly we may be remembered;
   The reflections of our souls thus measured.

How well we succeed in doing these things,
   They mirror and define our paths.
It is by these that we chart our destinies;
   It is we who compose our own epitaphs.

Time

Time...life...
   How we live it is up to us.

Time...life...
   When will we learn
      To live it as we must?

Time...life...
   Before we return to dust.

"The Edge" Revisited

Here on The Edge,
   I've looked down into the depths,
      Up into the sky;

Deep, so deep,
        In my friends around me
                In life where I pass by.

Life immortal,
        We here are stricken;
                Touch the act I play.
People, be it known
        You are not alone;
In the wind, pass by today…
        My world, on The Edge.

You may think me mad,
        But even I do not know
                The secrets I hold inside.
I run, see me run;
        My life, not yet done.
What I've done, much to do;
        That I dare to touch you.
                Do you care?
                        I do.

II. For the Heart

Quiet Love

To witness, to care;
> To promise to be there
>> When you need me.

Together at home,
> When needed, left alone;
>> It's all for you.

Quiet love, these days;
> You know there's very many ways
>> For me to show my love for you.

To continue as we are;
> Spirits near, passions far.
>> Quiet love; I like the way it touches me.

Home

Two lonely, frightened people;
> Living in a world unknown.
Now joined together, discovering friendship;
> Finding in each other a home.
Not being afraid to touch
> Or open up to their feelings inside;
Reveling in their sharing together,
> No longer having to hide
>> Their love for their worlds within.

In Perfect Love

In perfect love there is no fear;
    Imperfect love lets no one near.
In perfect love, we trust always;
    Imperfect love holds jealous days.

In perfect love, we are secure;
    Imperfect love, the heart impure.
In perfect love, the self is whole;
    Imperfect love seeks to control.

In perfect love, all held is shared;
    Imperfect love knows not to care.
In perfect love, compassion is wealth;
    Imperfect love knows only self.

In perfect love, all souls are served;
    Imperfect love, none else are heard.
In perfect love, our lives are blessed;
    Imperfect love knows no success.

In perfect love, we seek to find;
    Imperfect love only makes us blind.
In perfect love, we rest our hope;
    Imperfect love, it cannot cope.

In perfect love, we place our trust;
    Imperfect love cannot save us.
In perfect love, we give our all;

Imperfect love just makes us fall.

We're so thankful for that perfect love
       From which we're blessed from far above;
For perfect love, it gives us peace
       And joy and freedom and release,
              From the mortal and moral bondage
                     Of imperfect love.

Student of Life

For a child of God should know happiness
       To show and teach others,
And a child of God should know sadness
       To be able to cry with others.
And a child of God must learn to appreciate life
       Through all its highs and lows,
Understanding that it is in both that we
       Learn to be alive in our feelings and emotions.
Once learned, our humanity is strengthened,
       Enabling us to feel compassion for the fragile souls;
Not only those outside of ourselves,
       But as well for all that we are within.

Life is paradox, life is emotion,
       Life is tears, life is laughter.
Fill our lives with enough laughter to share with others;
       Allow tears to touch our lives so that we may stay human enough
              To reach out to someone else in need.

In this we can admit the truth before ourselves and to the world
   That we cannot do it alone:
      That we need our friends.

And when we are willing to admit that we need our friends;
   When we are strong enough to show them
      How weak inside we truly are,
Then they can show us in return
   And in the act of our sharing, may we find love.
For within all of us one of our deepest needs
   Is to find the love that we may receive from another,
And our passion…
   To have the opportunity to give just a little bit of ourselves.

Sadness and joy are as one in life for the student of love.
   In our living out of them we find the truth of life;
      Our desperate need for one another.
We can discover and experience those needs that we all feel within
   To the fullest limits that life allows.
All we need is to know that we don't have to do it alone;
   All we need to make our lives truly matter
      Is for us to every now and then,
         Be there for someone else.

When We Don't Get All of the Attention We Want

Love means little, if naught,
   If the one who we love
      Does not love us as much in return;
         The above is not a fair evaluation.

We know in our hearts that others do love
   If we are wise enough to see it.
      It shows in their own ways;
By their actions, in their words,
   And in those other myriad qualities
      That only those of great empathy can ken.

We can learn to be content in these which they are able to show,
   If we understand that its expression
      Is one within the harmony of their own souls
         In the time best given to us.
True in their words and deeds,
   These being the small and humble means
      Best available for some to show what they do have to give;
For not all have wells so deep,
   Nor passions so fierce as the fires we feel inside.

It is within the nature of our own humanities
   That we always desire more;
      This can be okay.
If it is truly love we feel,
   We can find the strength to temper our own demands.
To seek to be calm, to show we understand;
   To be thankful towards others for what they are able to show.

We should not unduly demand to confront them
   For their apparent lack of that which we crave to receive,
For that measure of themselves we may deem as insufficient;
   That paucity which they are genuinely and generously able to offer.
For it may be to them true to the people they are within

That they are only able to give but a small part of themselves;
For it is by the grace in which we receive that which we are freely given
That we may come to learn to treasure it all for what it truly means.

For what others may show us and that which we receive,
We don't always realize the great or personal cost that it takes for some
To be able to reach that deep within themselves to find…
That small amount (in our eyes) that they are able to give,
To offer unto us some small part of themselves
That they would be unable to show any other;
We are not to betray nor dishonor that trust.

Discover and embrace patience.
Understand and take comfort in the thought
That in the experience of any random moment;
Love felt, love given, love shown, love received,
Is almost always unequal,
Even between those of deepest relationship.
Rather, we should learn to be thankful for the all that is there.
If not, it is our peril that we in the end might lose
All that is and which we desire the most;
That companionship which we are so graciously offered or given.

Live for Today

Appreciate what is;
Do not suffer for what is not
Or for that which only could be.

To find things to appreciate
  They must be sought after;
    Our time is too short to be wasted, isolated to self.

Approach life boldly;
  Do not limit yourself through shyness,
    Unfounded fears, lack of trust,
      Lack of faith, or fear of rejection.
This can be done through a healthy love of self
  Shared unto others.

The happiness and peace that are centered within the self are not lost;
  They can be used to touch and change other people's lives.
    Sometimes these are gifts that are returned.
Self-happiness that centers around others is a fragile thing,
  And the person who exists as such
Lives in the constant fear of losing it
  And being broken.

True self-happiness can be discovered within;
  It can't and doesn't come from the outside.
    It is a gift that must be given to oneself.
To find it, learn to be bold;
  To reach out, to live life, to love life.
And above all else, to be able to forgive
  And to be honest and true to oneself.

III. From the Heart

Northern Lights

Northern lights
    Swirling across the sky;
Shining in the eyes
    Of newfound friends.

Wherever I go
    I find my family;
Waiting there with open arms,
    Ready to give security.
They welcome me
    With the smiles of those who know how to love;
        The northern lights shine clear.

The light that comes to be;
    See how bright it shines.
Wherever I go I always know
    It's waiting there for me;
        Love will always guide the life I live.

No greater joy can come to me
    As my days turn into nights;
Alone in the dark,
    What a sight to see,
        Those shining northern lights!

The Power

Oh, how sweet the simple power of a hug;
    The words unspoken in a gentle gaze.

I am humbled, so humbled, by the power within
 The hundreds of caring ways
  Others have shown their compassion for me.

Moments

Moments talk, moments touch,
 All I can say is it means so much;
  The warmth I feel so deep inside
   Whenever I think of you.

In these moments we show we care,
 In these moments we dare
  To touch each other inside;
   We share our friendship, our love.

These moments we now know
 Are but only for a while.
  In them I see your love for me;
   The kindness in your smile.

These moments we share today.
 They give me hope,
  They help me to cope
   With whatever life brings my way.

Moments come, moments go;
 What it is I want you to know
  Is how incomplete my life would be
   Had you never passed my way.

Attention

The touching gentleness in a simple word;
    A quiet voice of concern brightens up my day.
Aware of my needs, sensitivity…
    My heart feels happy and full of thanks.
Say hello, talk with me;
    My soul's appreciation is incomparable.
My all, it gives its thanks for such people;
    Gusts of gladness blowing over a cloudy heart.

For Love

Life is a kingdom,
    My heart a throne;
My will a servant,
    My mind makes a home…for love.
Time is the canvas,
    Touch is the color;
Words are my paintbrush
    Stroking another…in love.
Peace is the morning
    Endewed with a song,
The sun shines on brightly
    Forever on strong,
Where there is love;
    When I live my life for love.

Touch

The butterfly touch of your fingertips
    Lights upon my face;
The autumn breeze coolness of your voice
    Secretly steals its way into my ear.

Secrets pass between us;
    I read them in the voiceless lines on your face.
A thousand birds take wing in my heart
    When I find myself in the center of your gaze.

Cool mountain streams do not quench my spirit
    Like a gentle glance and smile from you.
Violn strings caress the air, melodies pure;
    But they cannot compare with you.

Time stands still; dawn approaches
    Never comes, in the moments we are together.
You touch me, I touch you.
    Comfort is knowing you'll never leave;
        Our love lives on forever.

These Eyes

In some eyes there lie
    The power of daggers and caresses;
Flashes of ice darts,

The face of a brick wall.
But in your eyes I see me
    And into your arms I fall.

Under the white flag of lost freedom
    No longer myself, my own;
Into your eyes I fall into me
    And with you I feel I'm home.

Can you see in my eyes
    The me I want to show you?
Help me, reach out to me,
    I no longer want to be just my own;
        I need to belong to you.

Looking into one another's eyes
    Deeply, tenderly;
Perhaps we can no longer
    Have to feel like we're alone.

Aria

Why has this obsession
    Come so over me?
The need to know you love me
    Is like a thirst never slackened;
And so I try to convince myself
    It's better to have none at all.

Sometimes it's me within I question,
   To convince myself my love is only lust;
For then I would have every reason
   Not to live it and let it be shamed.

But if it is simple love;
   As I want to believe, as I believe…
Why do I, me,
   Feel it so hard
      On you…you?
It seems so long I've been fighting this feeling;
   I now accept it.

It's been so long.
   I wish so hard, I wish I knew;
My heart, it hides from me,
   Keeping my mind in darkness
      And burning me so full.

Even when you've been gone,
   At the times I am alone
      With no one but myself,
You seem always to be with me
   Shining there so hard;
      Never letting go.

All I ask is for understanding
   And reassurance,
      To be allowed to be a trusted friend;
A shoulder in pain,
   A song in joy,

A someone in your life.
I care for you;
Lord knows how much
As I have yet to find the limits.

Even when we thought
We had done each other wrong;
All I tried to do to set things right.
As I was so afraid
That in the hollow ring of your empty silence
The loss would be forever.

Whatever my prayer should be:
My only desire,
My only want,
My only need…
Is that somehow love will overcome
And I won't have to spend
Another day alone without you.

In truth, all I'm trying to say is that
You're a someone to me,
And if you ever have the need for a someone;
Let me know, why can't you see,
Why can't you just let it be me?
Because I care,
I really do;
I love you.

Your Denial of Me

I still love you; you no longer love me.
    Alone at night I shed not a tear because of the truth I see;
        I understand…your denial of me.

Revenge I do not seek, I have the power to make you cry;
    Your memories I keep next to my heart.
        Goodbye, farewell, my love…

Perhaps, someday, come in its passing, you will finally see
    That through our changes thick and thin,
        Lived on my loyalty.

Perhaps someday, again you will need
    A friend there at your side.
If such is to be, remember me
    And how I could have been there for you;
        Just like it used to be.

My love, it does not,
    It has not died;
        Despite your denial of me.

Frozen in Time

I think to move ahead,
    I feel held back with my past.

Knowing all too well my life's failures
    I seek to remove them from me,
        Never to revisit nor repeat them again.
I feel trapped in my life's dream;
    Unwilling to move forward,
        Unable to give back.

I believe myself to be frozen in time.
    Trapped, bound;
No way out,
    No escape to be found.
I dream, I despair,
    And still someday I hope to be offered
A hand to pull me in;
    A heart that can help me feel again.

Until then, I wait;
    Bide my time, drink my wine,
        And consider my life lived in vain.
My hope persists that someday;
    Someone special, a twist of fate,
        An unraveling of my chains
May allow my heart to feel;
    Some warmth to be rekindled again.

My desires: to shatter
　　This translucent pain that suspends my tortured soul;
For time to resume, to again know the joy
　　Of the broken remade whole;
To find some way to renew my hope
　　For a lifedream all my own,
To reawaken from their slumber past moments lived and known;
　　Secure within the loving arms of another.

Universal Need

Life, I live it day to day; who knows me, understands?
　　I need someone to comprehend, accept my heart's demands;
　　　　And there's no one there.

People, I watch them by and by; I listen, hear their pleas.
　　No one hears or seems to care; it sounds so much like me.
　　　　When we reach out, there's no one there.

We all want, we all need, we fall on our knees;
　　We strive to make our claim.
Know me, understand me, truly listen for a change;
　　But yet…there's something strange.

What we desire in our hearts so passionately;
　　We all too often fail to give to others.

Apart

We are apart, separated; and by more than just the miles.
You are my heart's true love; but, for a while, we cannot live together.
Other people I meet, they remind me of you
In the words that they say, in the things that they do;
I am lonely, I miss you, and I can't stand to be alone.

Forgive me if in my loneliness I am with them as I wish to be with you;
For such a promise I cannot keep, to be wholly faithful and true.
My security is in your loving arms, your tender kiss; but you are far away.
Please understand that I am alone, I might be led astray;
Sometimes I go crazy waiting for the day that I might see you again.

Understand, love, if something should happen, I don't love you any less.
I'm always here if you should call, my heart it will confess
That you are my one and only true love.
So turn not your heart against me, but in compassion look at mine.
Hold true to me that love you hold; perhaps someday in time
We may again be able to live and love together as one.

IV. Life Echoes

War and Peace

In search of inner peace and freedom;
    How to be content with our lives as they are?

The world, it seeks to steal our joy, fill us with despair;
    Misleads us as to what's important,
Feeds us lies about what to care;
    Tries to be our master as to how we all should be.

It seeks to have us at war with ourselves;
    Telling us what we have, what we are, are never "good enough."
To hell with it is what I say, we're the ones to judge what's true;
    More honest to ourselves in finding, who is me, what are you?

It's a far better thing to know ourselves
    Honestly and intimately, self-forgiving;
Half-price and on-sale fail to give us
    The self-peace we need for joyful living.

The truth is the answers we're given don't last;
    To learn to be thankful is a better plan.
To embrace all within, both the good and the bad;
    Simple it isn't, all that makes us human.

To be true to ourselves we make our stand,
    For inner peace, our own flags we must unfurl;
At times that means we'll disagree
    And struggle to find a common world.

For peace within, sometimes it's better
　　To stand our ground, be true to self;
If we need to be at war with the world
　　That we do, with or without help.

The important thing is that which we do
　　Is what we know to be honest and right.

The Most Precious Gift

Love should never be taken for granted,
　　Assumed to be there if we are ever in want or need of it.
It's most curious state,
　　Sometimes we don't learn until it's too late;
　　　　Once lost, it becomes most conspicuous in its absence.

What Is Love?

Love sometimes confuses us all
　　When we get caught up in its emotion;
One question is all we need to ask
　　When we're trapped by the commotion.
The answer is all too simple,
　　It's a matter of the heart laid bare;
Who is the one most dearly loved
　　When it comes to how we care?

The question is what we value
    In ascribing our true intentions;
Other's happiness and wellness, our first concerns,
    Or more coveted are their attentions?
Is it our desire to serve what is best for them
    Or are we more "in love" with the way that they
        Make us feel good about ourselves?

One path reflects if our love is true;
    The other only means it's all about you.
To be self-honest is what we need
    When it comes to this confession;
It's the best way to tell the real thing
    From infatuation or obsession.

I Met an Old Friend Today

I met an old friend today
    Who at one time I made hate me;
Unshaven, squinting in the midday sun,
    He looked well.
We talked of general meaningless trivialities
    Instead of how I had to learn to less love him.
I cut the conversation short, saying that I had to go,
    When I sensed that it was becoming too awkward and boring.
Neither one of us was willing to show
    What it was that we were wearing deeper within our hearts.

I know now that people can only stand so much truth;
 I now know that to fall in love with a friend
  Can be a dangerous thing.
Where is the line between need and greed?
 When is taking a friend's offered kindness
  A license to provoke their time and attention,
   Insisting to be the only special one in their life?

Another time, another place, I asked a friend
 To accept changes in me that were more than he could bear;
  He asked me to get out of his life.

Still yet again, a friend whose devotion I insisted on having;
 His companionship was never enough.
  With my ever-increasing infatuation, he grew to hate me.
In final desperation I was forced to hate him
 To exorcise him from my heart.

Why do my friends have more power to make me feel
 Than I could ever hope to influence them?

Love Incomplete

I give to you most all of myself,
 You give to me a hug.
In your gentle gaze I feel secure,
 But it's never quite enough;
  Friends can only be and do so much.

Wanting to Forget

We've both made our share of mistakes;
    We both cared and then over the years, learned not to care.
And our only wish now is to forget,
    To bury our memories in time.

But still it happened, that cannot be denied;
    Once we cared, once we touched, once we shared
As friends, as more than friends;
    We were in spirit as one.

But now, after all has gone so wrong, so very wrong;
    We choose to part our ways, but the memories still hang on.
The only wish now is to bury them, to recall them, never;
    As if it could be possible to forget our times together.
To be able to will each other out of our hearts,
    Out of our minds;
        To not recall forever.

Where Is Me?

Isolation;
    Wasting, watching the last precious moments,
        Die like embers, gray away.
In the middle of the dirty street
    I lay, weary down,

And try to sleep;
But the fear remains,
Knowing my life will end in tragedy.
Home, where is home?
Where is me?

Living out the ideals of others of who I should be;
In search of love,
I bend to the will of those
Who would be masters of me.
They push, they see,
They take; knowing I'm too willing to please.
Not having the will to resist,
I can't live as others do…
For me dead is as lonely.

When will I find the courage to stop them
Before they steal my soul?
Will I ever know the feeling;
What is it to be whole?
Well, I don't know.

In the middle of the dirty street
I lay weary, down, and try to sleep;
But for me dead is as lonely.
So I live out the dreams of others
Of what I should be;
Of who I should be.
In search of love
I question what it means to be free;
Home, where is home?
Where is me?

Photo Album Memoirs

I recall the colors of the people of my past;
    Once vibrant and so full of life.
Now like the shadows of my memories;
    Old photographs mounted on the pages
        Of deep-closeted albums long forgotten.

Blurred outlines, faded colors, pale shadows;
    Over the years not attended to, substance lost.
The havoc time creates on that which once was whole
    Etches scars of days gone by deep upon our souls.

My memories are now but images fragmented,
    Pleasant reminders of the once familiar;
No longer recognizable,
    No longer held dear;
The people who once were
    The most important reflections of myself in my life.

Now fond and fleeting afterthoughts
    Of those moments in time when we once were;
Past reminders of glad fields, fully lush and green,
    Now pockmarked brown by our failures
        To offer them the due care which they so richly deserved.

Such is the price paid all too high
    When it comes to those once treasured;
Instead have now become
    The casualties of our emotional neglect.

Unrequited Love

I know you can't see me as I want you to;
    How could I make you care?
There's no chance, no way, no how,
    To make you feel the things I do;
And you've made it clear you won't accept
    The things I want to share.

To me you are so beautiful,
    The rarest kind of jewel;
Your eyes, they don't see or understand,
    And I stand here, just a fool…needing your love.

But you can't, you don't know how
    To touch me as I want to be touched.
Why can't you understand
    Just how deeply, just how much,
        I need you to be as one with me?

Over a Beer

Through brown glass they stare at their pasts
    With thoughts of those once held dear.
Look at the proud, silly men;
    Unseeing, staring, through their beer.

Remembering hearts and times forgotten
    Through the yeast and water rotten;
From the eye into the malt
    Mixes time and watered salt.

We Will Meet Again

Our lives are like the winds and tides.
    I change you; you change me.
Through these times of passage we've come;
    Yet deep inside we still feel the need
        For each other's presence in our lives.

Times hard and soft we've shared;
    Our road, so short and yet so long.
It's nice to know that we still care,
    Still keep a common bond;
        That has lasted us our whole lives through.

Now upon our roads has come the need,
    The time to say goodbye.
It's hard for me to say these words,
    To somehow not to cry;
        It's so hard.

And yet I have a comfort,
    For me you're always there;
In feeling your light shine on me,
    In knowing that you care,
        Enough to hold me as a friend and not let go.

And so I say there will come a day
    When our paths will cross again;
And we can talk and share
    Of when and where
        Our lives have led us, then,
We can reflect and partake
    And peruse what to make
        Of what we've come to be;
Challenges endured, our friendship assured,
    We'll be able to share and see
Where life has changed and taken us
    Separately...together.

V. More Reflections on The Edge

The Edge — Interlude I

I run, see me run, my life not yet done.
    My world, insecure;
        My lifesteps, unsure.
In a world so familiar
    I look at my mirror inward;
And I see a blur, just a blur,
    Of once when I knew
        What I was…who I was.
In desperation,
    I cling to The Edge.

Search (The Edge — Interlude II)

Life exists but I do not.
    I have been dead to myself and the world around me.
        I live, but I do not live.

I know from where I have come,
    Yet I do not recognize where I am.
I do not know where I'm going;
    I must find out.

Here is The Edge, I face myself;
    I'm not sure I like what I see,
        But nor do I understand.

I must search to find my destiny;
But before I can do that,
I must search to find…
Me.

The Edge and Me

Today I am on The Edge.
Today I am bared before myself;
Reflecting, conceding,
To my heart's eternal quest
Ever forward leading.
The future, the past, it's all so unclear;
I shuffle, I pause, it's now and it's here
I stop to look at the mirrors inside my world.

Here alone, to confront;
On The Edge, in the hunt,
To find in the depths
The reality of me.
It's a moment that's sometimes feared,
Not desired;
A need exigent,
Time required,
To sink into the deep silk darkment of my soul to find
Those parts of me which must be found
If I am to go on to my tomorrow.

Looking back on my footsteps

In the solitude of night,
I look back behind myself to see
　　The pale images of light
　　　　That mark the paths of where I'd gone before.

The images, they shine, but they're all so unclear;
　　They mock the winding roads
　　　　That through time have led me here.
Ahead of me lies the dark firmament bare
　　Of any landmarks, signposts, or talismans there
　　　　To be my guide.

Here is The Edge, I face myself; what do I see today?

The future, a tremendous gulf before me;
　　Beckoning, insecure.
The past made up of fading footsteps;
　　Reminders of past endured.
The present, the beckoning of desires;
　　Promises to be fulfilled.
But my steps, my feet are steeped in dreams,
　　So as not to move, unsure;
Unsure, unsure,
　　Where can I go if my footsteps are unsure?

Here is The Edge, I face myself; what do I see today?

Understanding, understanding…it eludes me;
　　Life sometimes, seeming too much to bear.
I look, I see so much emptiness,

But also there is fullness everywhere;
    If I would but only look for it.

Love, it is the guiding light;
    Truth, the road to follow.
        Peace in heart can ease the nights of loneliness and sorrow.
But weakness of spirit threatens, the fullness ebbs and flows.
    The promises of life, they come slowly;
And the yearning always grows
    To be more than that which I am.

The Edge, it beckons, it calls me;
    While on it the world stands still.
But life goes on, as must we all;
    It is time our steps must fill.

My life, not yet done;
    I run, see me run.
        Will I run, can I run?
Yes, I must; yes, I must.
    I will.

Twenty-two

Time passed ago,
    Once a part of me;
Past worry for the future
    Now has come to be
        A lie.

Tomorrow lives only for itself;
    What must come will come to be.
Today is the day that must be lived,
    With no thought of my future I am free…
        To be me.

The times that have passed I keep;
    The time I live I hold.
The time tomorrow lives in hope,
    And in the love we share lies the gift of gold
        We all so desperately seek.

One footstep follows another
    And forward I will go.
The time is now to live and learn,
    To laugh and cry and grow;
To make the most of every day
    So tomorrow I will know,
That I will have lived my life
    Content.

Now Fifty-nine

Down into the depths,
    Up into the sky;
These places on The Edge
    Define our lives as we pass by.
Love in all its forms;
    Every kind of pain we're shown.

In plenty and in dire need,
    The seasons we've all known.

Every moment lived on The Edge
    Brings us closer to ourselves.
All that we've endured;
    Our heavens and our hells.
The truths that have scarred our souls,
    Self-honesties past due;
The helpful guides who've shared our paths
    And helped to get us through;
        We've all had our share.
In our minds, in our souls, in our hearts;
    They never go away.

Myself, I've filled my cup with victories
    And worries of today;
Future doubts, they come and go
    And try to block my way;
Reflections of Edges past and present,
    Remembrances that inhabit my soul;
I welcome each with open arms,
    Their presence keeps me whole.

In the deepest places of myself
    Where they join with heart and mind;
I'm glad to say they bring me balance,
    Remind me to be kind;
Enabling me to ever stay...
    Thankful.

VI. The Rest

Aftermath

Blood on leaves, smoke on the breeze,
 From the now dead sound of forty automatic rifles;
Jungle green, blue sky serene,
 Lie to the passerby birds of peace on earth.
  Death here is the only reality.

Lost echoes of guns, lost mothers' sons,
 Not even Papa is here to caress the progenial brows.
Boys here have died, it matters not which side;
 A passing tapir grunts her stern disapproval
  At the twisted forms that do not here belong.

A face in the mud, his last gurgle of blood;
 Fleeting thoughts of his comrades, gags the taste of red beer.
Hears their calls in the wind, seeks not to join them,
 But soon they will welcome his company.
  Ghosts can laugh, too, can't they?

Day slips into night;
 With loss of thought comes loss of fright.
  Look, the maggots have come to enjoy the feast.

To the Mountain

And I beheld a voice inside me that said, "Yea, truly, it is time for you to go up onto the mountain."

Inwardly, I cringed at the thought, for the mountain was the place where only the angels who walked among men could go. Within its heart resided the source of the highest spiritual wisdom; and in its essence, it was the realm of the ultimate truth of life.

I could not bear the thought, as I knew the depths of my own uncleanliness and unworthiness.

Inside, I longed to return unfettered to my world of no inhibitions and every free choice, where there was no right and no wrong; simply being, feeling, acting, reacting. I reveled in the freedom of having all things being open and available to me, without the fear of responsibility or consequence. But inwardly I knew the trap before me; there I had long existed. Meaningless was its substance, and I was all too familiar with its seductive snares of reckless action devoid of any personal reckoning, knowing all too well that my evasions of accountability for the detritus of the feckless decisions of my past were merely pretty and petty tableaus for the trappings of my inner rationalizations and stagnation: empty, hollow and vain.

I needed, I wanted better, but didn't know how.

Again, I heard the voice, "Go! Come before the mountain!"

In my vision, my sightless void of darkness in which I tread, I saw a vague form in the distance; a pulsing, living blackness looming, encroaching, threatening to surround me. Within my spirit, my awareness increased as to its essence and purpose: to distract and divert me, to mire me in my own sense of dissipation; left to languish without hope or goal, coercing me to occupy all of my time and energy in the pursuit of the vacant, vain, and fruitless; enticing me so as to draw me into itself.

"Go!" again boomed the voice.

I raised my eyes and I saw

Light.

From the peak of the mountain, a beacon of light searching, arcing towards me, offering promise and hope.

Then the full moon broke, bathing all in a shadowed, sickly veil. The visions of nameless forms rose up all around me; many of them I knew well.

"Stay," they said, enticingly, mockingly; "stay and play, and all these promises will again be yours."

"Go!" again trumpeted the booming voice.

I cringed there, motionless; frozen, listening, wondering what to do.

I looked again to the mountain, wistful and despondent, feeling the searing iciness of tears, unexpectant and desperate, wet against my lips…

And wept.

Dare to Dream

A child steps into growing, his life's dream;
    As a man, comes to face his destiny.
Along the way he loves, he learns;
    Along the way comes pain, his turn.

But yet he's not afraid, he knows the power of love.
    Yes, it hurts and it binds, though sometimes unkind;
        He believes in its power above all other things.
And so he dreams, continues to believe in things unseen;
    He'd been hurt, now he's clean.
        His heart will rise again; he dares to dream.

A special someone walked into his life, his dream;
    They as two, came face to face with all life had to be.

Along the way they loved, they shared;
  Along the way then somehow, they learned how not to care.
But yet he's not afraid, he knows the power of love.
  Yes, it hurts and it binds, though sometimes unkind;
    He believes in its power above all other things.

As all things in life move in circles
  There will be another time; this he knows.
    Through all of our joys and sorrows, we grow.
So he looks from now to some future day;
  Believes in love, it will come to stay,
Patient for its return;
  He dares to dream.

Yet, he's not afraid, he knows the power of love.
  He's been there, no longer naïve,
    Knows all too well the road may be rough;
      Still…he dares dream enough.
He knows the odds against him, but secure with the love in his heart;
  Still persists in believing for his come someday dream,
    That he will find a love that will never part.
Dare we all to dream.

Blunt Instruments

Look deep into the mirror if you dare.
  Look inside, within the lair
Of the beast that roams the mazes of your mind,
  Of your soul; who knows
    What lies in surprise wait for each of us there?

Good, evil, sorrow, joy;
    Look inside a man and find the boy
        Who fears the steps to take; the plans to make.
Who knows where this man goes
    When his heart outspeaks the truth
        His mind doesn't want to hear?

Words, blunt instruments;
    Desires for unfulfillments
        Torment the haunted man-child deep within his lair.
Words, blunt instruments;
    Are the face of those rare moments
        Of unflinching truth encounter souls are bared.
How fragile can be a man's sense of being
    When honesty must always be conceded;
        Sticks and stones pale when compared.

Blunt instruments, how precarious;
    Blunt instruments, they can bury us.
Every man's pride eclipsed inside;
    Sometimes there's nothing left to do but hide
        For men are not often given the freedom to cry.

Too many real selves struggle, long to shed the tears;
    Yearn for some way to feel free.
Instead wasted away are the years;
    Endless striving for ways to shield their fears
        From the force of those blunt instruments;
Jagged-edged thoughts concealed deep within,
    Which in painful silence forced to endure.

Illusion

Players, on a screen of no return;
　　Breathing life as seasons burn
　　　　And the fortunes of a future never told.

Kingdoms, of molten polished brass;
　　Ever retained with sealing wax
　　　　As the dust of blinded past rises nevermore.

See the power enter ruin
　　As the werewolves storm the moon;
With the good man on a trip
　　And the bad man jumping ship,
　　　　Can you hear the people praying in the dark?

The spark of life
　　In dreams, in souls;
　　　　Desires of a people, ever bold,
The hopes they've sold,
　　In trade to find the heaven they seek.
　　　　It's all illusion.

Long live the memory
　　Of the stage lines half forgotten;
　　　　The life that once had meaning.
They have found the truth,
　　It's all illusion.

Prideful Man, Wise Man

Prideful man, arrogant man;
    Is always too sure.
Others are the ones that make the mistakes,
    His rightness ever endures;
        Considers himself above the rest.

Humble man, wise man,
    With his ever-questing mind;
Knows there's always more to learn,
    New things he can find;
        Ever alert for the different, not afraid to be second guessed.

The prideful man treasures only that
    Which he can name his own.
The wise man embraces other's thoughts,
    His mind for them a heart and home;
Keeps that which is of genuine value,
    Has the wisdom to throw the rest away.

Seasons of Learning

Some people have an air of infinite sadness about them;
    It shows in their eyes, they know the lessons learned
        In life, in love.
They've been there to see the seasons burned
    And risen again.

They wear the scars of wisdom, of battles lost and won;
        They have fallen on their knees before the moon
                And have stood proud before the sun.
They know the magic of love and the turmoil of storm;
        The cold blue frost rimed loss of heart,
                And the fires of touch held close and warm.

They have faced all these things
        And learned to smile at each new day.
Through chaos times, truth and lies,
        Stronger, they've learned to survive;
A little older, a little wiser,
        Having made profit of the lessons learned.
And within the passions now held in their hearts,
        Hides the longing need of their yearning
                To pass their wisdom onto others;
So that we, too, can grow proud and true
        And come to appreciate our own seasons of learning.

Young Man, Old Man

Young man, alone,
        You search on for a home;
You wish upon a dream
        That someday could come true.

Old man, days passed;
        You knew it wouldn't last.
You wish upon another star
        And hope it shines for you.

If all of us would ever see
    That if our love is going to be,
We must let it start
    From within our hearts
        And share it out to all.

Young man, old man;
    Believe it if you can.
There will arise
    Love in your lives;
And once you've found it,
    You won't have to feel alone anymore.

Old Man's Dream

A picture screen, an old man's dream;
    The flickering images of life
        Pass by before your eyes.
A lonely tune to the pale night moon
    Rises with the wind,
Flows with the tears you hide;
    Reminds you of the memories held deep inside.
        Old man; don't cry.

Thinking back on long ago
    Wishing we could know,
        That the life he's led has somehow touched us all.
Through fields of green this old man's dream

Plays to the setting sun, a life not yet done;
Wrinkled hands holding
The glories of his past,
The lessons hard won.
With a heart full of fear and warm eyes sincere
Touched with the mists of love,
He passes them onto us
Hoping that we may someday understand.

This life, so long, like a passing song,
Like the old man we know, will end.
For it, like we, who guard the old man's dream,
Can only begin to grow, and don't you know;
That one day it is we who will look to the setting sun,
Think of what we have done,
And dream…an old man's dream.

Afterword

What does it mean to be "On the Edge"? This is a phrase commonly found in our society and, depending on the context, can be interpreted in a number of many different ways: individual and situation dependent.

This concept, as interpreted in my writings, has both similarities and yet some very different connotations as to this phrase in its common usage.

The intent as to my original poem, written in 1979, was an observation on a certain life process that we all periodically go through. What occurs as a part of this is that frequently we all become so preoccupied and distracted by the very act of our day-to-day living, that we fail to notice within ourselves the internal changes we go through as a result of the events and interactions we have with the people around us as these occur over time. This continues on until we reach those moments in life when (for any of a number of reasons) we are called upon to have to take a serious and honest self-evaluation of ourselves: how our paths have led us, where we are now, and to take stock of what the future might hold. These are times of (sometimes precarious) self-reckoning.

As to when and why these happen, the causes are varied; sometimes these are marked by events which bring about significant life changes, and for those who are more inclined towards introspection, these times can be simply just an exercise in periodic self-maintenance. An "On The Edge" moment can frequently occur under times of great stress provoked by changes in one's life (as examples, relationship problems, loss of job, etc.) or not. Sometimes, being "On The Edge" can feel like a not very pleasant experience because we may be called upon to have to explicitly explore places within ourselves that we dread, sometimes even fear; but then again, this does not always have to be the case.

The common factor in all of these is that we are compelled to make a deeper-than-usual—as honest as we can make it—evaluation of ourselves, our relationships, and our lives; not always a pretty picture.

As to the poetry itself, this book is divided into two distinct parts. The original draft manuscript of "The Edge" was first compiled in 1982, primarily composed of poems written over the previous five years, with some additional new works written and added in order to provide some sense of continuity, cohesion, and to apply more of a storytelling format. It is the alert reader who will notice the growth and maturing process that occurs, along with the changes in voice as the story unfolds.

To start, I will note that this is a process that is mostly representative of a specific life phase and maturity level group (roughly age 16-26), although the life circumstances, emotions, and thought processes involved within can easily occur at any age. I specifically mention this grouping, as it reflects the actual relationships, adventures, and misadventures that I had the opportunity to claim firsthand witness to and experience all too often in myself and with my peers during those particular years of my life.

The narrative starts with the representative central character; the not quite yet fully matured young adult encountering life's emotional realities. As events unfold over time, and as life and the sense of his/her own self-identity unravels, a questioning as to all things occurs, especially as to one's own life and all of the big questions that at one time or another we all ask ourselves. As the story of the quest for self continues, starting with Witness I, enter the compassionate and caring friend who serves as a guide through the rough patches. What follows then in rapid succession is a period of resolution and affirmation and by the time Witness II is completed, this searcher

158

and learner has now grown and developed to become more of both a life student and teacher, feeling both a passion and an obligation to pass on the wisdom learned to yet others. The remainder of "The Edge" then develops into an appreciation of "life's lessons learned" of sorts, reflecting on the various elements encountered, and finally arriving to a place where there is a resolute and confirmed sense of purpose; a place where substance and life meaning have been attained, and to offer a place of rest and respite from where all these life adventures have led.

For the reader to assume that this is a profoundly autobiographical accounting of my own young adulthood, that is completely correct. However, it is also much more than just that, as some of the poems reflect not only my own life but that of several of my good friends and other relationships that I've had both the joys and sorrows of living with over the years.

It is also important to keep in mind perspective (especially with much of the earliest work), as to trying to relate to the high levels of immaturity, emotionalism, desperation, and obsessions as they are lived through and experienced by youth, adolescents, and young adults. That is, until (like all of us) they finally enter the realm of their own more mature, reasoning elder selves; that point where most of us eventually reach. That being said, as an older adult now, I embrace the fact that I've been quite fortunate to have lived the life that I have (even with all of the ups and downs) and have finally wound up at a very good place in my own life. I now view myself as being very much at a place of self-peace as to the world, my own life, and with God as I understand Him/Her to be.

As to my contemporaries and those younger, I still see a lot of the same kinds of struggle that I endured within some of them, as they strive to somehow find a way to come to a place of self-peace within themselves. My intent is that for those who are still encountering these types of dire difficulties with life and self, that my writing may offer a sense of hope as to what may lie ahead and that which could be (especially given the context and high level of my own past insecurities and anxieties as reflected in the early chapters).

As to the remainder of the book, I prefer to consider it as a continuation of the learning and growth process; adding to that "more" that we encounter as adults. After all, these are processes that if we are wise, we understand that these never really end if we are to develop into our fuller and fullest potentials.

Some may wonder as to why I've chosen to add all of this as an Afterword rather than a Foreword. The reason is simple enough; I think it's a better choice to have my readers form their own impressions and ideas as to the poems and stories as they unfold without any antecedent clue giving or prejudice instilling commentary or interpretations on my part. My desire is to have the words speak for themselves so that everyone can extract specific meanings and emotions for themselves upon first reading.

To be sure, some phrasing and verses are specifically designed for open interpretation and to offer the possibility of having more than one meaning; some verses I don't even completely understand myself. I consider this as all part of what makes for interesting (and hopefully good enough) poetry. I believe that writing should be like any other form of artistic expression; the work is crafted in such a way that suits the artist's own good pleasure and which reflects one's own essential heart and passions. If it so happens that the work is found to be appealing and is able to inspire feelings or emotions within others, or if any should like and appreciate the innate artistry of the craft on its own merits, then so much the better.

To finish, self-peace to all, and I hope that you enjoy the reading as much as I've enjoyed the writing and sharing. (Do you have a question or would like to make a comment? The e-mail address uncommonpoemscommonpeople@aol.com has been opened for this purpose; my sincere and heartfelt thanks to all of you).

T. D. Kruser
November 2019